FEARLESS AND DETERMINED

Two Years Teaching in a One-Room School

a memoir

Linda Hutsell-Manning

Fearless and Determined
Copyright © 2019 Linda Hutsell Manning
All rights reserved
Published by Blue Denim Press Inc.
First Edition
ISBN 978-1-927882-43-6

This is a work of non-fiction. Permissions have been obtained from real-life persons mentioned within. Fictional names have been used for those we have been unable to contact.

Cover Design by Robert Scozzari.
Front Cover photography by Star Weekly
Back Cover photo: Judy Baker, photo taken by her aunt Jessie Pratt (deceased)
Typeset in Windlass, Cambria and Garamond
Library and Archives Canada Cataloguing in Publication
Title: Fearless and Determined : two years teaching in a one-room school : a memoir / Linda
Hutsell-Manning.
Names: Manning, Linda, author.
Description: First edition.
Identifiers: Canadiana (print) 20190140933 | Canadiana (ebook) 20190140976 | ISBN 9781927882436
(softcover) | ISBN 9781927882443 (Kindle) | ISBN 9781927882450 (EPUB)
Subjects: LCSH: Manning, Linda. | LCSH: Teachers—Ontario—Hamilton (Township)—Biography. | LCSH:
Rural schools—Ontario—Hamilton (Township)—History.
Classification: LCC LA2325.M36 A3 2019 | DDC 372.110092—dc23

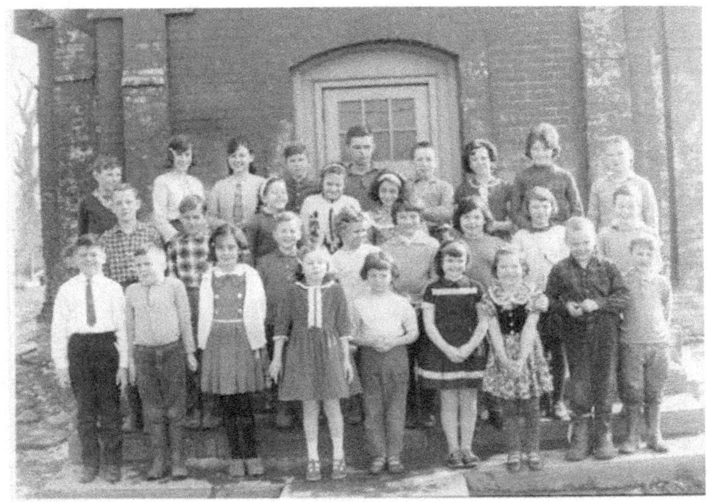

"An 'old school' memoir of the nicest kind - and Linda has excellent penmanship as well." — **Ted Staunton**, author 50 children's books, the latest, *The Almost Epic Squad.*

"In *Fearless and Determined: Two Years Teaching in a One-Room School,* versatile writer Linda Hutsell-Manning effectively transports readers back to an era of galoshes, Freshie, stencils, cap guns, and gunny sack races as she recounts—with visceral clarity—her 1963-1965 teaching term in a one-room school. In her tripartite role as sole teacher, secretary, *and* principal, having 'so little time and too much to do' was her constant reality, and with a toddler at home, 'working mother's guilt' often lurked in the shadows."— **Shelley A. Leedahl**, multi-genre author, the latest *The Moon Watched It All*

Other Works by Linda Hutsell-Manning

<u>Novels</u>
Jason and the Wonder Horn
Jason and the Deadly Diamonds
That Summer in Franklin

<u>Plays</u>
The Adventures of Freddykid and Seagull Sam
Merch the Invisible Wizard
The Great Zanderthon Takeover
A Certain Singing Teacher

<u>Poetry Juvenile</u>
Wondrous Tales of Wicked Winston

<u>Television</u>
Five scripts for TVO's *Polka Dot Door*

Table of Contents

Foreword

Recounting my two years teaching at SS#2, the Front Road School West has been a fascinating journey into the past. Certain incidents that I have recorded, I remember clearly while others, I do not. In the course of working on the manuscript, I interviewed many of my students and was told about situations, either, I didn't remember or knew nothing about. During my first year teaching, the students and I created a Yearbook, detailing not only information about each student but also describing all notable events that took place in our one-room, ungraded school. The second year relies on my memory and student recollections. Without student and yearbook resources, I doubt I would have attempted to write what has turned out to be an amazing journey to a time and place, most who read this will never have experienced.

Where I have received permission, I have used students and others real names. Where information could be sensitive or controversial, names and identities have been changed. These latter incidents are included in the book as they are representative of situations taking place in one-room schools in many farming communities leading up to and including the 1960's.

There is, of course, an aspect of creative non-fiction in this memoir: dialogue in most instances, as well as situations I had no memory of fleshed out to become real events. These additions knit everything together and move the memoir forward.

In many ways, teaching in a one-room school in the 1960's differs little from teaching in this same environment since one-room schools first appeared in Ontario. My school was built in 1860 and would have been considered modern by many one-room school standards of that time. It was brick with six big windows; pit toilets were installed inside the front door, a step up from the more traditional outhouse; and there was running water inside, a cold water tap and sink, certainly more convenient than an outdoor well and pail of water. Even though, by 1963, the physical premises of The Front Road School West had deteriorated, most students who attended, accepted it as the only school they knew, this one room where learning began in grade one and continued until the end of grade eight.

I have included, at the end, both an Afterword and an Appendix. The Afterword comments on the striking differences in teaching methods between the 1960's and the present while the numbered Appendix gives, in more detail, specific aspects of teaching and the curriculum.

Year One: 1963 – 1964

"There are some things one remembers even though they may never have happened."
Harold Pinter *Old Times*

"The past scampers like an alley cat through the present, leaving the paw prints of memories helter-skelter."
Charles de Lint *The Onion Girl*

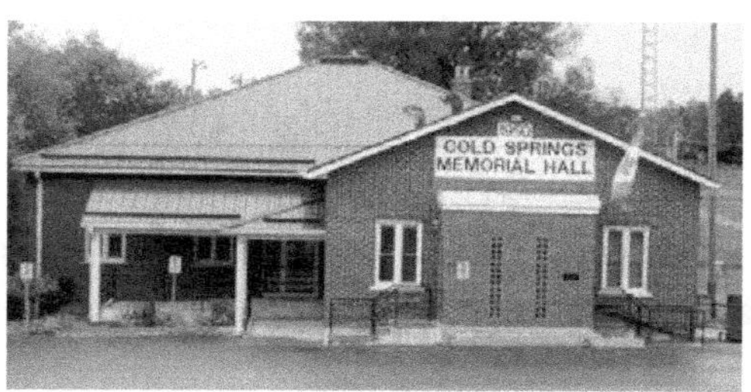

Photo of Hamilton Township Hall 1950's (*From the archives of The Corporation of the Township of Hamilton*)

The Interview

On a hot day early in July 1963, I sit nervously on a straight-backed chair in a narrow, airless foyer of the Cold Springs Hall. I'm waiting to be interviewed for a Hamilton Township teaching position in a one-room school between Cobourg and Port Hope. For those of you not familiar with the area, these are two small towns on Lake Ontario east of Toronto. My two previous interviews for Cobourg town school teaching jobs had been unsuccessful. My interviewers were not impressed that I had turned down teaching right after Teachers' College to be with my new husband, whose job posted him to northern Quebec. Before applying for this job, I had no idea one-room schools still existed, especially in southern Ontario. Teachers' College, a one year course with only minimal classroom teaching, has given me no practical preparation for such a job. I don't care. I need to teach two years out of five in order to obtain my permanent teaching certificate and, as I have spent more than two years travelling with my husband as his job moved, I know time is of the essence. The most practical plan is to live in our hometown, Cobourg, and stay with my kind mother-in-law,

Rosamonde Manning who has offered to look after my one-year-old son, Bruce. This job interview is my last chance at teaching in the area.

The young woman beside me looks definitely younger, likely right out of Teachers' College. She goes in ahead of me and my anxiety increases expeditiously as the minutes tick by. She is back out sooner than I expect and looks neither pleased nor discouraged. When I hear my name called, I stand, determined to be calm. The not too spacious Board Room is in dark panelled wood, a long table down its centre. Seated around, looking weathered, some still in their barn clothes, are the Hamilton Township Board Members.

"Mrs. Manning?" a man at the end of the table asks, a bit gruffly it seems to me.

"Sit down, sit down," someone else adds.

I sit in the end chair, acutely aware of six, or is it seven, sets of middle-aged male eyes scrutinizing me.

"I see you graduated from Toronto Teacher's College in 1961," the man at the end begins.

"Yes," I manage before my throat constricts. I know what the next question will be.

"And you didn't teach for the next two years as you went with your husband, James Manning, to Northern Quebec," another man adds.

I nod, feeling my face reddening. The town schools did not take kindly to this information. Rather, they seemed to hold it against me as some deficiency in my moral character.

"That would be Russell Manning's son?" someone else pipes up.

I nod again.

"And what would this husband of yours be doing in the wilds of northern Quebec?" a Board Member near the end of the table asks.

I can't help wonder what this has to do with my teaching ability, but dutifully reply, "He was installing computers in military bases on the Pine Tree Defence Line."

They seem impressed by this, nodding and making notes. I am beginning to feel a little like Alice and I know I have not fallen down a rabbit hole.

"Do you have any experience in a one-room school?"

"Not directly," I reply, "but I did attend Baltimore Public School from grade six to eight and was in the senior room of the two-room school there."

"Miss Hogg," a man sitting opposite me, barks out, slapping his knee. "Now there was a crackerjack of a teacher."

"She taught in this very school," the man beside him adds.

"She did that," another replies. "1957, I think it was."

More note scribbling. At this point, I want the interview to end. I can't see what this has to do with my suitability as a teacher for this school.

There is a momentary lull and I consider, for a second or two, jumping up and bolting. Am I so unsuitable that they are asking random general questions, nothing about how I would handle a given discipline situation or what approach I would take to a particular subject?

"Mrs. Manning?" The man closest to me is staring, tapping his index finger on the table. "Didn't you tap dance at the Baltimore Community Centre?"

I nod, feeling my throat tighten again. This is beyond ridiculous. "A long time ago," I manage to say. "The Judy Welch School of Dance."

"You were real good," he adds.

More scribbling.

I wait, feeling sweat running down my back, inside my girdle and, I'm sure, staining under my arms.

The man at the end of the table stands up. "That will be all," he says. "Thank you, Mrs. Manning."

By the time I am in the car and on the highway, tears blur my vision. I blink furiously and pound the steering wheel. I don't want to teach anyway. I'll find something else. Another job. Who needs teaching?

A week later, a letter from the Hamilton Township Board arrives at my mother-in-law's. I have the job. Duties of the first school year are to begin Tuesday, September 3rd 1963 and end Friday, June 26th 1964. Remuneration is $3000 a year, with an extra $300 because I will be both teacher and principal of this one-room school. Although this amount seems ridiculously low by today's standards, it was double the average Canadian wage.

After my initial euphoria subsides—I'm going to be a teacher with my own class, all eight grades of them—I refuse to be intimidated. I will figure it out; how to teach eight grades at the same time; how to prepare and organize lessons for umpteen courses starting with a lesson plan or plans. It has to be doable even in the eight summer weeks remaining.

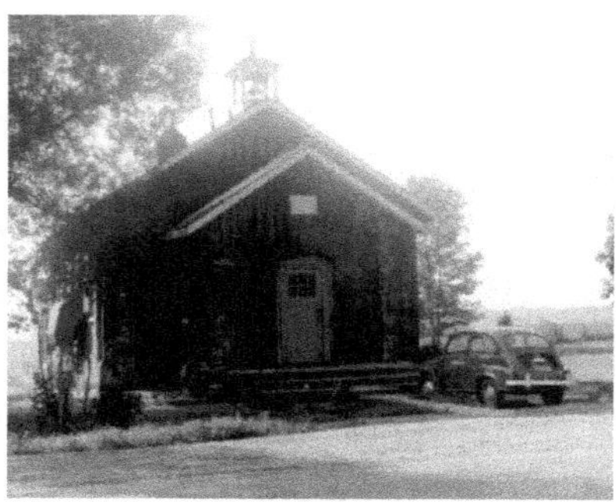

The School

The School

Shortly after the interview, my designated Board Member, Mr. Moore, phones and says he can meet me at the school. My mother-in-law has generously offered me the use of her car, a red Honda Mini. Mr. Moore says he will show me around the school and give me the key. I remember a rush of excitement hitting me: my school with my own key, such a lofty responsibility and, as I soon will find out, such a heavy work load.

We pick a day and time and, on another hot summer day, I drive along Highway 2 west of Cobourg, past the Golden Miller restaurant and its road north to the drive-in as he has instructed and, find the school on the left, fields on either side. A one-storey brick building with a bell tower on top and a wood shed behind, the school has obviously seen better days. It appears that some years ago, the brick was painted and now, in many places, paint has worn off revealing faded bricks, many of them weather-pocked.

Mr. Moore grins broadly as I step out of my car. "Welcome," he says, "to the Front Road School West." The pride in his voice helps diminish the unease I am beginning to feel. Eight grades in one-room. How will I ever manage? I follow behind through the front door, past two closed doors and a storage area, into the school room proper. Its lack of amenities remind me of pictures I've seen of pioneer one-room schools, a step back in time, almost like the TV show "Little House on the Prairie." The few schools I was in, during my teaching training year, were Toronto schools: two stories with a room for each grade, a staff room, an office and a generous foyer. Schools I attended as a child were much the same: the school in Charleswood, Manitoba where I spent my first four years of schooling and Baltimore Public School where I was in the senior room of a two-room school. The six large multi-paned windows are shut and a blast of heat hits us as we enter. As we pass through the narrow hallway into the main room, I can smell, but not identify, something decidedly unpleasant. "Pit toilets," Mr. Moore says, nodding back at them, "and don't you worry, the janitor makes sure they're kept clean during the year." Janitor, an outdated word by today's school standards but, yes, they were called that in the 1960's. "Mrs. Carr, one of your student's mothers is our first-rate janitor."

He stops beside a substantial wood stove a couple of feet inside the door. I eye the long black pipe rising at least twice my height to become horizontal, ending where a patterned tin rim protects the plastered wall as it enters the chimney. "Yes," Mr. Moore continues, giving the stove's black surface a pat, "our Mrs. Carr cleans the school twice every week, and one of her older sons comes early mornings in winter to get the stove going."

He goes on to say that wood is stored in the shed behind the school and that there is always a good supply. The stove sits on a tin base separating it from the worn plank floor boards, a box for wood on one side. Everything is in pristine condition, not a stray ash in sight. I imagine it will be different in winter, stray bits of bark strewn on the floor, ash coating the base beneath, possibly strewn further out onto the wood floor. I wonder who stokes it during the day.

"If you're wondering who tends your fire during cold days," Mr. Moore says, as if reading my mind, "it's one of the senior boys. No need to ask for a volunteer, they all know it has to be kept stoked." He rubs sweat from his forehead and runs his hand over his pants. "Hard to imagine on a day like today!"

I smile bravely and nod. Pit toilets and a wood stove. What else?

The sink. I hadn't noticed it, being so absorbed by the long expanse of pipe from the stove. Rectangular porcelain in shape, the sink sits in a cabinet on the back wall, beside a linoleum-topped table with weathered legs. An ancient-looking tap arches over its pocked interior, a long, reddish-brown stain beginning from where water hits the porcelain, ending at the partially rusted drain cover. "Cold water tap," Mr. Moore says brightly and, as if it's an added bonus, "a pencil sharpener."

An ancient bookcase stands against the east wall, its books looking as though no has touched them in decades. Large slate blackboards rise up between each of the three tall windows on both sides of the room, with the front wall entirely covered by their dark surface. They have been washed and gleam black in the light coming through the windows. I am, at least, pleased with the windows. Without them, it would indeed be dark and dreary. Little do I know that there are no storm windows and that, in winter, when the wind blows from east or west, delicate piles of snow will collect on their sills.

The desks range from small in front, to large at the back, the small ones being the kind you slide into from the right with a wooden writing surface extending around to the front, a drawer under the seat. Half way back, these become desks with chairs and a flat surface for writing, a shelf beneath. I assume the different sizes carry with them status by age, possibly grades one to four in the more contained desks and grades five to eight in the larger ones. I wonder what happens if there are too many juniors and not enough seniors, in which case small children will be sitting on chairs too big for them, or, if the reverse, larger seniors will be obliged to squeeze into desks too small. I keep all this to myself as Mr. Moore shows me about the room.

The teacher's desk faces the student desks, close to the front blackboard. It's made of solid wood with a centre drawer and two side compartments with doors. I sit gingerly down in the worn wooden chair behind it. It has arms and is on wheels. Again, I feel a rush of power? Responsibility? Whatever it is, it quickly diminishes, again, to apprehension.

Mr. Moore throws a key onto the desk. "I'll just let you stay here and find your bearings," he says. "Need to get back to my chores." He gives me a little salute and strides out, slamming the door behind him.

I sit, staring at the blackboards, the stove, the bookcase, the sink: everything run down, un-kept or just plain old. It's obvious the Board doesn't have much money, if any, for building upkeep. "Never mind," I say aloud. "You have a job, a whole school of your own. So get at it." I pull open the centre drawer and discover a large, black hardcover attendance register.

Inside the front cover, is a list obviously written by the previous teacher. There will be seven in grade-one, three in grade-two, six in grade-three, four in grade-four, six in grade-five, three in grade-six, three in grade-seven, and one in grade-eight.

I will the queasiness in my stomach to leave and think back, briefly to my Teachers' College year, the worst year of my life. I found it humiliating; Miss Belfry who taught us primary skills and was obviously a former primary teacher herself, gave us each a printing book into which we were required to print the alphabet letters, both capital and small. Matronly in shape with a coiffure of stiff blue hair, she was fastidious in her appraisal of our printing, circling in red any part of a letter that didn't align precisely. I was always in a hurry and thought the whole exercise to be ridiculous. As a result, I almost failed printing. As I try to come to terms with the enormity of the task in front of me, Miss

Belfry's blue hair and my wretched printing book momentarily strike me as incredibly funny. Its significance was paramount at the time, given I could fail the subject if I didn't toe the line, while now it seems a mere speck compared to preparing all subjects for eight grades.

I get out of that lovely teacher's chair and pace around the periphery of the room, my tread echoing ominously, dust whirling up into incoming sunlight shafts. When I realize I'm not even sure what subjects I am required to teach, I sit down again to search for a list, an indication, some vague help. What I find is a box containing pristine unfolded report cards containing, of course, a list of all eighteen subjects. I try not to panic. How can I possibly manage reading, spelling, literature, arithmetic, history, science and art to all these grades?

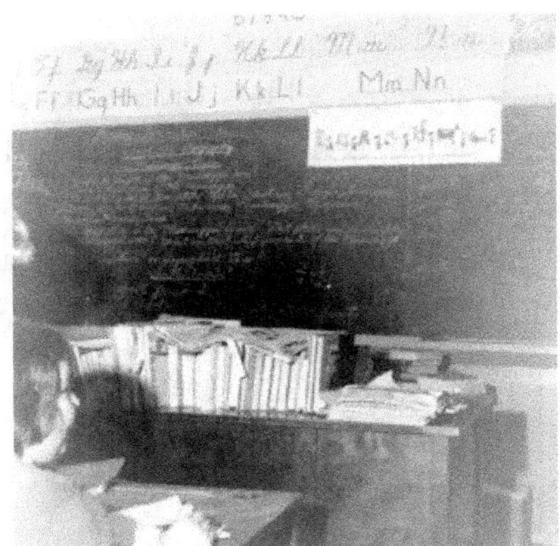

My desk

The First Week

I do remember, like it was yesterday, wheeling onto the cracked cement pad in front of the school, turning off my car, hoping my hair was in place and my blouse tucked in, clutching my purse and briefcase while attempting to gracefully exit the vehicle as thirty pairs of eyes stared at me, their gaze scrutinizing me. Guessing my age?

"Good morning," I remember saying, keeping my voice steady with a certain degree of authority.

"Morning, Miss," a chorus answers back.

I try not to rush, inserting the key in the lock, opening and closing the door. I don't even notice the pit toilet smell. Several windows are open and morning sun pours in from the east. The day before, I spent four or five hours, writing out seat work on all the blackboards, going over my class notes for the umpteenth time.

Three weeks before school began, I came to the school every morning and often into the afternoon to work on class preparation. One morning, I arrived to find a sealed box of new text books for grades seven and eight. The Department rules have changed and, this year, I am obliged to teach history and geography as separate subjects to grades seven and eight. I have two students in grade seven and one in grade eight. Because of this, I have asked my board member if the grade eight student could be moved elsewhere. I argue that it is unfair to her: no classmates, no reference points of comparison in learning ability. I'm also thinking of the work load, preparing a whole slate of lessons for one student. I have been told it is likely she will be moved but receive no official notification until the morning of the second day when her brother, Wolfgang, tells me she has been transferred to another school. It's going to be a hot day and, by the time I check my desk and my teaching notes, I am sweating profusely. I take hold of the bell by its clapper and march resolutely to the outside door. I have decided that strictness will be my mantra. I will not tolerate noise or whispering or rudeness or anything. I did not fare well with discipline during my practice teaching sessions in Teacher's College and was always criticized for being too lenient. Better to err on the strict side and, once order becomes the norm, then let up a little. Maybe.

The students are already lined up when I open the door, little ones in front, older students in a row behind. Their stare is unnerving, and I hold my head high and say firmly, "Thank you for lining up. No talking and no pushing. You may enter the classroom." I realize I have no idea who will sit where and am relieved to see, as I enter behind the last student, that they are slipping into desks, most likely the ones they had last year. There are eight new students, one of them being my sole grade eighter. As I make my way to the front, there is total silence. The newbies stand off to one side, waiting.

I have already printed my name on the blackboard and, nodding to it, say, "Good morning class. I am your new teacher, Mrs. Manning."

"Good morning, Mrs. Manning," they chant back.

I notice, then, empty desks, some at the front and some farther back. "New students in grades one to four, please take the empty seats near the front and older students find a seat further back." They slip into place, and the morning begins.

"Please stand for the National Anthem." I take out my pitch pipe, sound the note and begin singing. A few sing, several decidedly off key, a large number stand and stare. I finish my solo and go on to the Lord's Prayer. This is better although many of the little ones, obviously don't know the words. Something to work on.

I bark out orders, telling grades four to eight to begin with math and spelling and then go on to the seat work on the boards while grades two and three are to study the first story in their reader; I tell my six grade ones to colour the letter A that I am handing out to them. A is for apple, I say, not worrying that this is mundane or boring, keeping my eye on everyone, making sure they are all getting to work. When a hand shoots up with a request to sharpen a pencil, I say, "I know the sharpener is difficult, do your best and walk quietly." To say the sharpener is difficult is a gross understatement. It's almost impossible, grinding each pencil unmercifully, breaking the lead over and over. It seems this student and others who follow have learned how to deal with it. When a grade two student goes to sharpen her pencil, an older student slips in and takes over. I am impressed by their obviously practised co-operation.

When two older students begin to whisper, I hush them, saying they are disturbing others. Throughout the morning, they remain amazingly quiet. When twelve o'clock arrives and I announce lunch, a grade six girl raises her hand. "Are we allowed to talk during lunch?" she asks.

"Of course," I reply, "but do be courteous of others. No shouting. You can do that outside." Several heads nod and most whisper during that first lunch day. Within fifteen minutes, they are all outside and I am left with four piles of books to mark. Rosamonde has packed me a lunch, but my stomach is churning so that I can't eat.

A few minutes later, two grade-six girls appear and introduce themselves as Marilyn and Susie. Marilyn says they will help me mark. As they sit down, each taking a stack of books, Susie adds that they did this for the teacher before me.

"You should eat your lunch," Marilyn says. "You don't want to starve." I watch them settle in to marking and it's obvious they have done this before.

"I do appreciate this," I say, relaxing a little. "I wasn't quite sure how I would get them all marked."

After a few more minutes of paper turning and pencil marking, Susie says, "Would you mind if we put the radio on?"

"There's a radio?" I say, looking around.

Susie jumps up and, stepping behind my chair, produces a radio. "It was on the bottom shelf," she says, and then a little tentatively, "The teacher before you wouldn't let us play it."

"It's fine with me," I say. "Help us pass the time."

She turns it on with the sound so low, it's barely audible. "I think you'll have to turn it up a bit," I say, "or else we won't hear it."

"You're sure?" she replies, still looking a bit doubtful.

I reach back and turn the volume knob so we all can hear. The Beatles are singing, "She loves you yah yah yah," and Marilyn sighs audibly. I smile and the two of them begin singing along, marking and, often, turning pages in time to the music. I wonder if they are paying attention but, later, when I check several of the scribblers, all is in order.

This will continue, five days a week, during the entire school year. Often Irene in grade seven joins them, the three of them marking and singing, the Beatles' tunes being the most popular. Years later, having forgotten this, I always wondered how it was I knew all the lyrics to many of the Beatles' songs. My students, along with thousands of other preteens and teens, were Beatles' fans and their young voices singing with such enthusiasm was contagious. I don't think I ever joined them out loud but the lyrics, without my realizing it, were imprinted in my memory.

I decide during my lesson planning marathon in August, that I will read a chapter from a novel to the class on Friday afternoons after lunch. Finding a suitable book turns out to be a major challenge. I realize whatever I read will likely be over the heads of the grade ones and possibly the grade twos and I also know I have to find something with sufficient plot and interest to keep the intermediates and seniors interested. With some trepidation, I choose *Treasure Island* by Robert Louis Stevenson. It was first published in the late 1800's as a serial in an English children's magazine and, due to its popularity, soon after as a book. Given there are thirty-four chapters in the novel, I figure it will keep us going most of the school year. In the afternoon, seatwork for the seniors, science and history questions, is on the board. I ignore the fact that although several groan audibly, they all settle in to work. I begin an introduction to Social Studies, "Friends from Around the World," for the grade-three /fours. Insipid and stereotypical by today's standards, I read from a text describing happy children in different geographical locations—Africa, China, the Canadian north, Italy, France, Spain etc., propping black and white drawings of each on the front blackboard. The students are then to pick one or two of these to colour and print sentences about. I set them up into pairs, a grade-three and four together as the writing skills of the latter are substantially advanced from their younger counterparts. My two grade-two's and one of the grade-one's have listened intently to my presentation and then ask if they can colour one of the pages once finished their own work. This becomes a pattern in most of the grades as the year progresses: younger students listening in and, often, participating in a lesson of a grade or two ahead.

The rest of the grade-ones are looking through old magazines, finding, cutting out and pasting samples that match the picture at the top. For a picture of a kitchen, for instance, they look for dishes, food, appliances etc. Being as busy as I was, I didn't notice until they left for the day, that one student has simply cut magazine pages randomly, slicing them into twos and threes and fours, some even ripped. These are glued haphazardly onto the three sheets each student was given. No name is on this work and, as the grade-ones have not yet mastered name printing, I have no idea who it is. In the next few days, this mystery will be if not solved, identified.

The end of the day comes soon enough, the sun now pouring in from the west windows, most students putting books away and getting ready to leave. I have not, as yet, assigned homework. I want to wait and see how my students deal with a few days' assignments, how careful they are, whether or not they complete what I have asked them to do.

As soon as I stand and announce, "Class dismissed," they are up and out the door, not as quietly as when they entered but in a reasonable fashion, given it's the end of the first day. Once they are all gone, I am left sitting at my desk, feeling the proverbial hourglass sand sifting out of me. I have survived the first day.

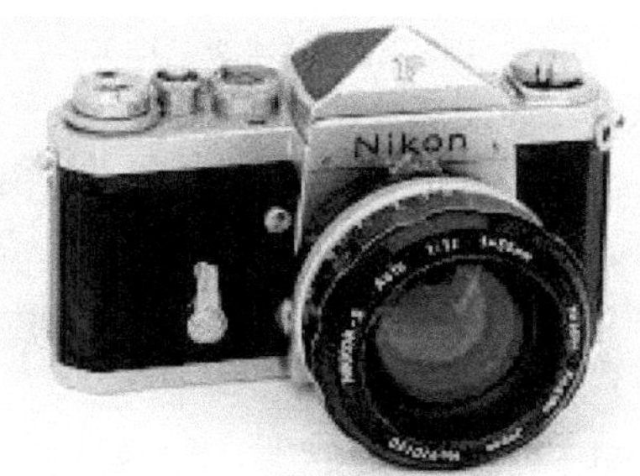

Nikon cameras 1960's

Unwelcome Visitor

On a Monday morning, the second week of school, September 9th, I arrive at school just after 7:30 a.m. to begin filling the blackboards with seat work for grades four to eight. I am hampered somewhat as, on the weekend while attending a wedding, the car door closed on my right thumb. I am thankfully left-handed but, still, find my bandaged thumb a painful impediment. I plan to have the seven grade-ones practice printing the letter "b" in their printing books. (Appendix 1) I was a bad printer in grade-one, back then, repeated again in my Teacher's College ordeal. I determine, therefore, to be somewhat lenient with messy printers, telling them if they can manage to be neater, printing words will soon follow and be more interesting.

I have one first-grader who is happy to colour pictures as all the grade ones have done the first few days of the previous week but, as soon as I ask her to print letters, she cries, great heaving sobs, as if I demanded of her something highly embarrassing or impossible. Her name is Kim and she has curly brown hair and big Raggedy Ann freckles. She makes fists and rubs tears away as they stream down her face. Reasoning with her, does no good and so, being as busy as I am, I let her colour. This will be the third day of printing for the grade-ones and the others are now considerably ahead. I decide I will give her a page to colour first thing and then, later, when one of the senior girls has finished her morning's work, have her give it a try. I nab my three noon hour markers as they are coming in, and Marilyn agrees she will work with Kim.

I step outside at nine A.M. sharp to ring the school bell. My charges dutifully hurry in, the older children herding the young ones in first. Once settled, the class stands to sing "God Save the Queen" and repeat The Lord's Prayer. I can't play the piano and, after the first two days of sounding the pitch pipe and having barely anyone except me and some loud off-keyers sing, Cathy Burnham, a grade-four student, offers to play. This greatly improves participation and the off-keyers are thankfully drowned out.

I have given the grade-ones printing instructions, with my freckled Kim happily colouring; the grade-threes are reading in preparation for my hearing them read out loud and I am beginning a phonics lesson with the grade-twos. An unexpected knocking on the outside door at first startles and then annoys me. Who could it possibly be? I'm certainly not expecting anyone. It's nine-fifteen.

I am still in my overly stern mode and, frowning at the class, I tell them to sit quietly while I answer the door. I march to the back through the short hallway between the pit toilets and, with some apprehension, open the front door. Surely a school inspector wouldn't be here this early in the term?

A neatly bearded man stands in front of me, two cameras hanging from straps around his neck. He grins and pushes his hand toward me. "Michael Lambeth," he says. "I'd like to come in and take pictures of you and your class. It's for an article in *The Star Weekly*." My thumb is throbbing at this point and I can hear muted whispering behind me.

I glower at him. "This is a one-room school," I say coldly. "I am responsible for these children and we are very busy. I can't possibly let you in, and, if you want to talk to me, you'll have to wait outside until recess at 10:30." I shut the door without waiting for a reply. *The Star Weekly?* I don't think so. I hope he will go away and wonder if I should requisition a couple of my senior boys as bodyguards.

Over the next hour, I sit with my three grade-twos, going over two of the different sounds the letter "Y" makes such as in "baby" and "cry." The grade-ones finish their printing and are happily colouring, except for Kim who howled even more loudly when Marilyn and then Susie tried to start her printing. They give up, shrugging their shoulders at me, and I nod to just let her colour yet again. I manage to hear each of the six grade-threes read, some finding it so easy and some struggling with every word.

At 10:30, I announce recess and everyone hurries out. It's a warm September day and the gnarled old tree west of the school is beginning to show yellow in its leaves. I have completely forgotten about Mr. Photographer and am busy marking grade-one printing books when a senior student sticks his head in the door and calls that there is someone waiting outside to talk to me.

I rush out into the glorious morning, more than a little rattled but mostly annoyed. "You're still here," I say curtly. "What would you like to know?"

"How many grades? How many students? How long have you been teaching?"

I answer as quickly as possible. I'm more interested in getting back inside to finish my marking. He scribbles down my comments and takes hold of one of his cameras. "It's a human-interest piece," he says as if I'd asked, "and so I'd like to get some shots of you and the children with the school in the background." He marches a short distance across the grassy yard, toward the sagging baseball diamond backstop and beckons me to follow. This is my first time outside at recess and I stand momentarily watching the children, some playing tag, a number in small groups chatting, a couple of boys tossing a baseball back and forth.

"If you could move a little closer to me," Mr. Lambeth calls. "Two more steps should do it."

I look at my watch. It's 10:35. I will be behind in my marking and who is this guy anyway?

"I only have another five minutes," I call. "And I must go back inside."

"Just a few more," he says, moving closer. I wish he wouldn't as I know I have a blemish on my chin and, if this wretched photo is going to be published, I don't want it to show. Also, there's a breeze and I can feel my fine hair flying every which way.

"Finished," he says, striding up to me. "Thanks heaps. Your name?" He pulls out his notepad again.

"Mrs. Linda Manning."

"Name of the school?"

"SS#2 the Front Road School West."

"The article'll be in the November issue," he adds, and giving a broad wave I assume is intended for the children, races to his car, and is gone.

I quickly forget the incident and might or might not have mentioned it to anyone afterward. I'm too busy preparing lessons and keeping ahead of the endless marking. I am surprised when the picture appears and realize my suspicion of this Michael Lambeth wanting to take a photo of us was ill founded. Although I didn't much like the photo, friends and neighbours do, being impressed my picture was in a Toronto newspaper.

Nearly four decades later, when I was updating my writing website, I decided it would be interesting to include the *Star Weekly* photo. In 2005, the internet was not nearly as easy to navigate, as now, but I did manage to discover Michael Lambeth was no longer alive. His sister kindly gave me consent to use *The Star Weekly* photo which was part of his estate. I later spoke to Maia-Mari Sputnik at the Art Gallery of Ontario who had published a collection of his photographs. She said there might be copies of the book left at the Stephen Bulger Gallery in Toronto. When I called there, they had one copy only. I drove in that day to pick up the book and feel privileged to have it. Lambeth worked for the *Star Weekly* in order to pay the rent and subsidize his art photography. I wish now I had let him come inside my school. I have only a few photos and my memory to recreate most details of the space.

When I look at the photo, now, I think how young and fresh-faced I was. I can identify some of my students in the background with the little red Honda close to the school. I think I parked it there instead of in front of the building, so the kids had a paved area on which to play hopscotch or skip.

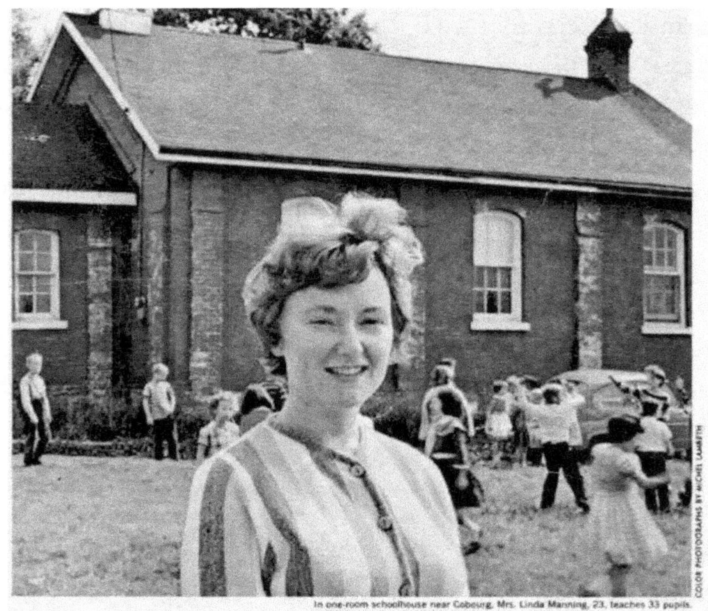

In one-room schoolhouse near Cobourg, Mrs. Linda Manning, 23, teaches 33 pupils.

Star Weekly photograph

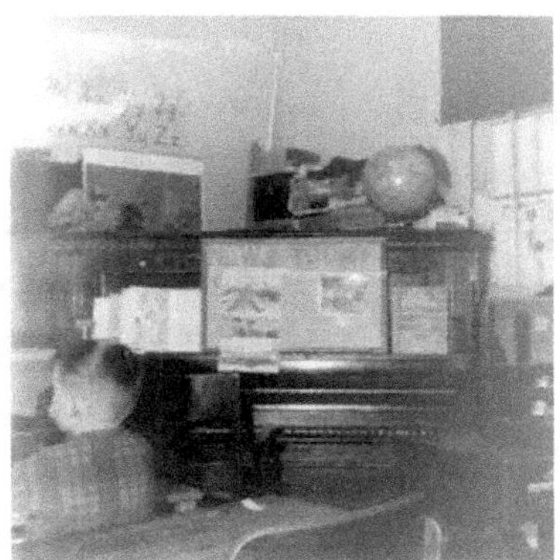

Piano in school

The Music Teacher Arrives

I know a music teacher will come to the school once a week but am not aware on which day this will occur. Music, which can be pushed aside even in a graded school, is substantially more problematic in a one-room school. Because of my keen interest in the subject, I am determined to give this subject its full two curriculum hours a week. From what my senior students have told me, Mr. Thrip will come for one hour, and that in the past the school population was divided into two groups, with one group taking an extended recess while the other was being taught.

When the outside door opens on a hot September afternoon and a man carrying a large briefcase enters, everyone stops working.

"Mrs. Manning?" he says, coming forward. "I'm Mr. Thrip, the music teacher." He places his briefcase on the piano bench and turns to the class. "Good afternoon, class." Everyone replies on cue, "Good afternoon, Mr. Thrip."

"You have several new students I see," he says, and I'm impressed he can remember last year's students seemingly at a glance.

"Six grade ones," I reply, "and seven in higher grades transferred from town."

He nods and continues, "For those who are new, I usually divide the grades into two groups." He stops and pulls several music books from his briefcase. "Today, however, we'll all stay together. I always do tone-matching to get things started. Could you play for me?" He nods in my direction. "A C chord to start."

"I'm sorry," I say, feeling more than a little inadequate. "I don't play the piano."

He looks surprised, perhaps a little annoyed, but says nothing as he sits down at the piano. "If you could supervise the children then," he says. "I'll start with the grade eights and work down. One student at a time, please, up here to my left, facing me."

"No grade eights this year," I tell him and, to the class, "grade sevens please, one at a time." Irene and Joe make their way to the front, a resigned look on each face. Irene's voice is clear and quite strong; Joe's has started to change and some of his notes are definitely not melodic.

"One Canary," Mr. Thrip says, nodding to Irene, "and one Bluebird." Joe shrugs but doesn't seem perturbed. I'm familiar with the Canary/Bluebird method of dividing children into singing groups and, although I do not agree with it, I say nothing. Mr. Thrip is considerably more experienced than I am and, if this is how he divides my singers, I'll go along with it, at least when he is present.

As the testing progresses, it's obvious that most of the unfortunate bluebirds, especially the younger ones are, to some degree, tone deaf. Several of the grade ones are frightened and don't want to take their turn. An older sibling steps in and escorts each to the piano. Kim opens her mouth but no sound comes out and, after Mr. Thrip asks her several times to sing, she starts to cry. "You can be a bluebird for now, miss," Mr. Thrip says, patting Kim's shoulder. "Next."

Once everyone is tested, Mr. Thrip says, cheerfully, "We'll now sing a few songs from last year. I'm sure you'll remember the words. Canaries sing out. Bluebirds clap the rhythm." This is moderately successful except that a number of the younger clappers get carried away and clap enthusiastically out of rhythm. Each time this happens, Mr. Thrip stops, plays a bar, speaking the rhythm—one, two, three, one, two, three— before starting again. It's a bit chaotic, but he doesn't seem to mind.

"That's all for today," he says to the class, and, looking at his watch, "I'll be back next week, the same time, for two of our regular sessions."

I dismiss the children for recess and Mr. Thrip waits for me to return to my desk.

"This is your first year?" he says, looking around the room. "You seem to have taken charge."

"I'm enjoying teaching," I say. "The students are delightful."

"If I could give you a word of advice," he says, nodding at the piano. "It would greatly further your career as an elementary school teacher if you learned to play the piano."

"I'll definitely keep that in mind," I say. "Thank you."

He nods and briskly exits. When would I have time to learn piano? I know Rosamonde's sister, Genevieve, whom the family calls Tante, plays well and could likely teach me, but, since every evening after putting my young son to bed I spend two or three hours writing out seat work in preparation for the next day, it would be impossible. I wonder why piano playing was not mentioned during my interview. I feel suddenly in over my head, doing a job I'm not really trained to do.

I remember grade eight at Baltimore Public school and the young itinerant music teacher, Mr. Ramsay, who, with my teacher, Miss Hogg, taught us a number of Gilbert and Sullivan pieces. We put on an abridged 1951 version of the *Pirates of Penzance*. I started piano lessons that year with Mr. Ramsay, and had I stuck at it there would be no problem now. Ballet and tap were more important to me then, and I rarely practised. I'm not sure I even lasted a year.

Each week, Mr. Thrip comes through the door with a cheery "Hello class and how are we today?" greeting. My students dutifully put away whatever they are working on and sit hands together ready to sing. After a few weeks, when I observe that my normally well-behaved students are less than attentive, I decide, given my inexperience in teaching, not to butt in and discipline offenders. Instead, I scrunch down in my seat, put the largest book I can grab in front of me, and try to mark spelling or math during the music lesson. The younger students are reasonable but some in the older group, continually agitate, using tactics I remember from my teacher training days. The first couple of times, I write down the names of the most blatant offenders and call them up for questioning after Mr. Thrip is gone. When I mention uncivilized behaviour verging on rudeness, the culprits, almost always boys, stare at their feet looking abject and uncomfortable. And usually, one of the girls speaks up to say, "But Mrs. Manning, it's so-o boring." After lecturing several weeks in a row, I simply ignore the hour as best I can.

The senior grades, which he teaches first, warm up with several scale sequentials. Having sung in a number of choirs, I am familiar with this exercise. Mr. Thrip plays a four-note sequence on the piano and asks the students to repeat it. Thankfully, a number of my students have good singing voices and, with the first sequential they sing the notes with gusto. He plays the next note that raises the sequence a semitone and asks the students to sing it unaccompanied. The first few times he does this, only the bravest students sing the new sequence. He seems surprised and a little annoyed by this and plays the remaining sequences with them. I make a note to practice this during the week.

After these scales, he picks a song from the *New Highroad of Song* and sings it in its entirety. He does have a good tenor voice. After, when he asks how many know the piece—and only two or three raise their hands—he says they will learn it as an observation rote song. This turns out to be similar to sequentials in that he goes through the song once, singing a line and having the children repeat it with him. At the end of the first run through, he checks his watch and briskly announces that the lesson is over.

"I'm sure," he says, taking the song book from the piano, "that Mrs. Manning will finish teaching this song and you'll all know it by next week."

I ask the page and name of the song, scribbling it down as he tells me. "Yes," I say confidently, "we will know it by next week."

At this point the seniors file out and the juniors, now heady with their extra-long recess tumble in, giggling and being generally close to out of control. I hush them and again introduce Mr. Thrip. He seems more relaxed with this group, but still tries, with only moderate success, to have them sing sequentials. He follows this with an easier song from *New Highroad of Song*, taught in the same "listen and repeat" mode used for the older group. As it turns out, the bluebirds have some inbuilt need to be heard, and so, the first time through, they blast out each line in varying degrees of monotone. He remedies this by segregating them and asking them to be listeners. As he goes through this song several times with the Canaries, the Bluebirds, as might be expected, react as only six to nine year-olds can: fidgeting, desk drawer opening, and asking to go to the bathroom. Again, I request the page and title and vow the children will know this song the following week.

During the week, I work on the songs as often as I can, often having two recesses and taking the groups separately for convenience sake. Our progress is slow but, week by week there is definite improvement. First thing in the morning and just before final dismissal, the whole class sings sequentials, the younger ones, following along where they can. As well, one or two of the senior girls drill the grades one and two at recess or noon hour. I create a Singing Chart on a sheet of Bristol board with juniors' names down the left and the dates practised across the top. We make a game of it and I promise a star for each student once I hear the group sing together. Ten stars and I promise a candy for each. Bribery? Yes. Bad for the teeth? Yes. Does it work? Yes! By December, a number of my young charges can sing the pesky sequentials fairly well.

Starting in October, on Fridays, I send the grade one to three's out for early recess and have a fifteen minute sight-singing class for grades four to seven. Mr. Thrip has told me he has so little time given there are eight grades and that many, here, are behind their age group in this aspect of singing. I realize it must be somewhat frustrating for him and, have been told by one of my senior students, that our one-room school is one of only a few in the township; his other schools are graded.

If the weather holds throughout the fall months, we'll have almost a dozen sessions to work on this new skill. We begin in the *New Highland to Sight Singing, Book Five* and work into Book Six. The great disadvantage to this is that a few of the older pupils do the actual sight singing and the rest merely follow. By late fall, there is, however, enough improvement to warrant Mr. Thrip mentioning our progress.

With this extended discussion regarding music, one might think it is all we do. But no, we carry on daily with all the other subjects. I am amazed and excited as, by the beginning of November, most of the grade-one's are beginning to read, haltingly at first, actually recognizing words and understanding short sentences. As well, many of the older students are making progress with math and English.

Some Struggle, Others Excel

In 1963, New Math was introduced to Ontario schools. An offshoot of a new program in the United States, this curriculum was designed to improve math scores for elementary and secondary school students. Thankfully, I had those few weeks in the summer to go through the shiny new text books and try to make sense of it. Having no teaching colleagues or anyone to advise me, I had to figure it out myself. What I discovered was, that the New Math breaks down most of the steps formerly used in solving almost every math question, especially in long division (Appendix 2)

I know that when using the old long division method, it has always been difficult for some students to grasp the "highest denominator" concept. I remember, myself, in grade three or four, trying out different numbers combinations until I found the one closest, the one that would be the correct answer. The New Math tries unsuccessfully, in my view, to solve this division difficulty.

A week or so into September, the grade-fours are required to do a series of long division questions. Near the end of grade three, long-division was introduced and so they have learned the old way. Now they must adapt to a new method. I go over it several times and I can see not everyone is catching on. Of my four grade-four students, one is absent, one catches on right away, one has a little trouble and one, I can tell, doesn't have a clue. An hour later, when they come up one by one to be marked, the results are as I expected. Cathy Burnham, who also has the advantage of knowing musical time, gets the fifteen questions correct. Allen Woodward makes a few mistakes while Karen Johnston only gets one, out of the fifteen, right. As I mark down her page, wrong answer after wrong answer, I sense her becoming more and more upset. When I mark the last question with an X, she bursts into tears. "It's all right," I say. "I'm not good in math either. We can work on this together." The poor child is sobbing now, tears running down her face. I give her a hug. "Don't worry. It's not that serious. We have all year to work on it."

She stops crying and says in a halting voice, "The last teacher would get so mad at me." She takes a deep breath. "Sometimes, she threw my book on the floor and yelled at me."

I vow, then, that I won't insist the children use the New Math. Those, who understand, will use the new method and those, who have trouble, will carry on the old way. There is no one to check on me and the end result will be the same.

After a few weeks, it becomes obvious to me that several of my students would be, in a graded school, called "gifted." Allan Burnham, in grade six, is one of these. Most days, he finishes his entire day's work by mid-morning and then sits quietly, hands folded, watching me and what everyone else is doing. There are no books in our antiquated library that would be of any interest to him, and his quiet nature does not lend itself to working with any of the younger children.

I decide I must create special projects for him and list a number of possible topics mentioned in the science and history texts. At recess, I show him these, and he picks two that he likes. He tells me his Mom takes them to the Cobourg library every Saturday, and he will look for books that will help him with these projects.

We agree he will write up an outline first to show me, and the following week, I'm impressed by his ability to look into a subject and find details and points to develop. By asking questions and getting him to develop points more fully, I manage to keep him busy with each project for several weeks. Once he has completed these initial projects, he comes to me with idea suggestions, and we work out more projects to keep him occupied.

His sister, Cathy Burnham, although only in grade four, spends times listening to younger children read and drilling them in spelling. If she and the older girls had not helped me in this way, I would be marking one or two more hours a day either after school or at home in the evening. We're beginning to work as a team, and, as the days pass, I realize I am really enjoying teaching, that most subjects are interesting and ultimately rewarding.

History, however, turns out to be the exception, the albatross of all my courses. No one except Allan seems to like it, and there are two reasons: the history books are at least twenty years old and the writing is archaic and boring. I can do nothing about either, and with grades four to seven I read through the textbooks, chapter by chapter and make up endless detailed questions which I put on the board. These exercises are make-work/give-me-time questions to keep the older children occupied while I teach the younger ones. I also hope having to write in detail about the content will help students learn it. This has only limited success. In retrospect, creating group projects would have been more interesting, but as there are no reference books in the school's limited library and no way to access the town library, I have made do with questions based on the wretched history texts. Continually, it is a matter of so little time and too much to do.

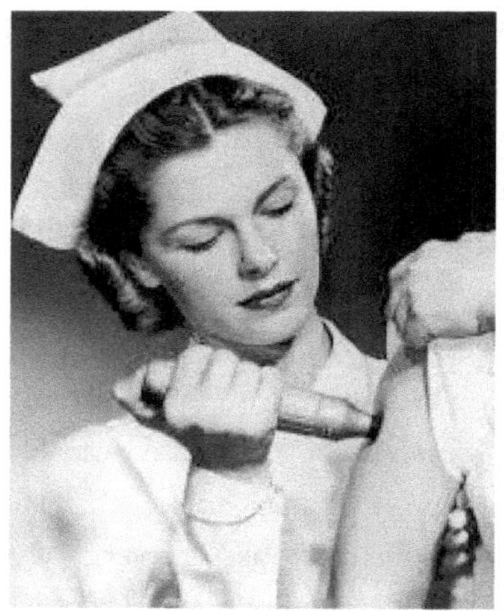

School nurse with smallpox needle

The School Nurse Visits

On Friday, after lunch, during the first week in October, several children rush in to tell me the school nurse has arrived. I am in the middle of marking grade-six math questions and not too pleased at suddenly being interrupted. I tell my noon-hour markers they are excused, clear my desk, and know I must be civil.

"I'm Miss Forbes," the nurse says, hauling in a large leather bag, with two of the senior boys behind carrying two smaller ones. "I'm giving immunization shots today."

She comes to the front to shake my hand. "Small pox and polio."

"I'm Mrs. Manning," I reply, taking the two pamphlets she hands me.

"One for each procedure," she says, "in case someone asks."

I put them on my desk, noting that her spotless white uniform and matching nurse's cap definitely give her that needed air of authority.

I suggest she set up on the back table near the sink and ask two of the senior girls to clear it and move it forward a little. Placing a white cloth on the tabletop, she begins to lay out her equipment.

Everyone is now back in their seats and I see that several younger girls are looking more than a little apprehensive.

"These shots," I say, holding up the pamphlets, "are most important and I'm especially glad everyone is present." I'm thinking particularly about the Stoaker children who have not been present for the past two weeks. "Small pox is a terrible disease," I add, "and many children in other countries have died after contracting it."

Cathy Burnham's hand shoots up. "Our mother's a nurse," she says. "We know this is important." This doesn't seem to have much effect on the malaise that has fallen over most of the children: pale faces, rapid breathing, some with heads down on folded arms.

"I'll give the small pox shot first," the nurse continues cheerily, "so I would like the children to line up, beginning with the grade-ones." She turns and washes her hands at the sink, drying them, I notice, with her own clean towel. She holds up a needle with two prongs. "I'll call each child forward in turn."

"All right, then," I say. "Grades one to four line up along here." I point to the aisle left of my desk. Several of the grade ones look terrified and don't budge. One by one, I take their hands to encourage them into line. Several older siblings come to stand with them.

Linda and Paul Burnham are bravely at the front of the line trying, I assume, to set an example. When the nurse calls, Linda marches to her and, holding her arm out, tightly closes her eyes.

"This is going to hurt a little," the nurse says, swabbing Linda's upper arm with rubbing alcohol.

I sit at my desk and scan through the small pox pamphlet. The nurse is using a bifurcated needle which is a narrow steel rod, approximately, two and a half inches long with two prongs at one end. It's designed to hold one dose of reconstituted freeze-dried smallpox vaccine between its prongs. The established technique is to dip the needle in the vaccine and puncture the child's upper arm fifteen times in a small circular area. The most effective vaccination will result in a small drop of blood running down the vaccinated arm.

Most of the children turn in their seats to watch Linda's face scrunch tightly as the nurse jabs the spot on her arm over and over. When it starts to bleed slightly, she dabs it with a piece of cotton batten and covers it with a Band-Aid, telling Linda she's very brave and may return to her seat. Linda does so, the hand of her unscathed limb holding the wrist of her wounded one, her eyes wide, mouth in a tight line. Paul is next, and he looks toward the window, lips set in a line, refusing to show any discomfort.

The line moves slowly forward, each child enduring what has to be done. Several of the younger ones sniffle audibly and, everyone post inoculation, looks miserable, many holding their wounded arms just below the Band-Aid.

With no warning Sharon Woodward, who has just been vaccinated, faints, crumpling down, her head barely missing the tabletop. The nurse manages to catch the child before she falls to the floor and, telling everyone to move away, turns Sharon onto her back. The nurse pulls a chair over in order to elevate Sharon's legs on its seat and, after checking that her clothing is not binding anywhere, asks for a glass of water. A moment later, when Sharon opens her eyes, the nurse feels her forehead and reassures her.

I rush to the back to provide a glass of water and wonder if there is anything I can do. "Should I see if she can be taken home?" I ask.

"She'll be fine," the nurse replies and, pulling Sharon's legs from the chair, helps her to a sitting position. "Would you like a drink?" the nurse asks, bringing her a glass of water. Sharon takes several sips and pushes the glass away.

"Maybe we should take a break?" I suggest. "We could stop for recess and carry on after."

The nurse looks around the room. "Good idea. But if there are any who want me to continue now, I will." The juniors straggle out, many still holding their injected arms. Before they've all left, Sharon asks to go with them. I ask another student to stay with her in case she feels faint again. The seniors, however, line up and most indicate they just want to get it over with. The line moves quickly, and, as each student receives a vaccination, he or she heads out to recess.

Once everyone is gone, the nurse gathers up the vaccination equipment. "Sorry about the child fainting," she says, "but it's not uncommon. If you look outside, you'll see everyone has recovered." I go to the window and notice that most of them are in small groups, talking and comparing experiences. "They're not as active as usual," I say, "but no one looks as though they're suffering too much."

"I always do small pox first," the nurse continues, setting a large glass bottle on the table. "The Salk polio vaccine, as you can see, is pink, and we serve it on a sugar cube. Children love it." She opens a box of Redpath sugar cubes. "This will be much more enjoyable. You'll see. Call the children in whenever you want."

When I appear on the step ringing the bell, the response is less than enthusiastic. Several little ones, in particular, hang back and refuse to get into line.

"You're in for a tasty treat," I say, beckoning the last few to join the line. "The nurse is ready to give everyone pink liquid on a sugar cube."

"Is it a real sugar cube?" someone asks.

"Absolutely. There's a big box of Redpath sugar cubes on the nurse's table."

This seems to revive the group and they traipse in expectantly. "This is almost like candy," The nurse explains, "a reward for everyone being brave." She holds up the bottle. "This is polio vaccine in a pink liquid." She exchanges it for the sugar box. "And I'm sure I don't have to tell you what these are."

"Sugar cubes," several voices chime out.

"Do we get more than one?" someone asks.

"Only one this time," Miss Forbes says, smiling. She nods toward me. "The same line as before?"

The juniors are quick to get in line, several pushing to be ahead. "Be polite," I say in my sterner voice. "Everyone will get a turn."

The polio vaccine on a sugar cube is a huge hit and, as each child sits, there is a prolonged candy-sucking sound, the needle terror forgotten.

"Back to work," I say, once the last student is seated. "I'll listen to the grade six and seven's read shortly; the fours and fives finish your Social Studies project and grade-three's, find your grade-one or two buddy and help them with printing or whatever they haven't finished."

The nurse begins to pack up her equipment, and I ask if she needs any help.

"I'll be out of your way shortly," she says. "It looks as though you have everything under control here."

"It's my first year, and, so far, I'm enjoying it."

"A heavy work load, though." She scans the blackboards filled with questions.

"I don't mind. The children make up for it."

"Before I leave, here is a list of instructions for small pox inoculation aftercare." She begins to count from a pile of papers. "Thirty in the class?" She hands a pile to me.

"Yes, but only fifteen families. I would like to keep the extras, though, in case some get lost on the way home."

She nods. "Could you go over the instructions before the children leave? They are most important." I ask two of the boys to help her take her things back out.

Before dismissal, I hand out an instruction sheet to the eldest in each family. "These instructions are extremely important. I want to go over them before you leave."

I begin to read, paraphrasing to a certain extent. Number one: in three or four days, if the vaccination is successful, a red and itchy bump will form where the needle punctured your skin. Someone calls out, "It still hurts, Mrs. Manning. It really does."

"I'm sure it will stop hurting, probably by the time you get home." I continue. "Number two: you must keep a clean, dry Band-Aid over the spot at all times. It recommends changing the Band-Aid, at least, every other day."

"What's a Band Aid?" one of the grade-ones, asks. Marilyn goes to the first aid kit on the back table and holds a couple of Band Aids up for everyone to see.

"My mommy says that's an owie fixer," another junior pipes up. A few giggles follow.

I'm wondering about households that may not have Band Aids. "When you come to school tomorrow, be sure to tell me if your family doesn't have Band Aids. I can provide a few extras." I make a mental note to buy a couple of packages on the way home.

"Number three," I continue, "it is most important to keep the spot dry. No baths and be careful when you wash not to brush the facecloth over the area." No one comments. "Number four:—during the first week, the bump will become a large blister that fills with pus and begins to drain."

"Yuk," a couple of female voices say; "Gross," someone else adds.

"This is important," I say. "It's how your body fixes you so you won't get smallpox."

"What is smallpox anyway?" one of the seniors asks. "I've never heard of anyone around here getting it."

I scan the pamphlet the nurse left. "This is what it is," and I read the definition given. "Smallpox is a serious infectious disease caused by the variola virus. It is highly contagious, meaning, it spreads from one person to another. People who have smallpox run a fever and develop a skin rash that develops into blister-like spots which break and run, causing the rash to spread."

"Sounds awful," someone says.

I nod and continue. "Most people with smallpox recover, but about three out of every ten with the disease die. Many smallpox survivors have permanent scars over large areas of their body, especially their faces. Some are even left blind."

"And this vaccination stops it?" Irene asks.

"Yes, it does."

"Then it's a good thing we all got this shot," Wolfgang adds. "No matter how much it hurt."

"There's a bit more I want to read." I look again at the instructions. Everyone is quiet, again, and I sense most of them now realize how important this vaccination is. "During the second week, the blister will begin to dry up and a scab will form. The scab falls off during the third week, leaving a small scar."

I know from stories I've heard and scars I've seen that the scar can be quite large, the size of nickel for some. The little needle indentations remain and it tends not to tan. I keep all this to myself as I hand out the instruction sheets.

"You are dismissed," I say. "Be careful not to lose the sheets."

Lunch pails and books are gathered up, and, before I take a couple of breaths, the room is empty except for my blackboard monitors. They don't say much and erase the boards more slowly than usual. When I ask if I should take over, they insist on finishing the job.

On the way home, I decide I will phone the doctor's office to find out when Bruce should have these shots. I know Jim and I had the Polio vaccine when we were living in Kamloops, BC, over a year ago. I remember lining up outside a large trailer and asking, specifically, if this was safe to take being pregnant. I must have been reassured as I know both my husband and I finished off our pink sugar cubes, smiling at being given medicine in this unorthodox manner.

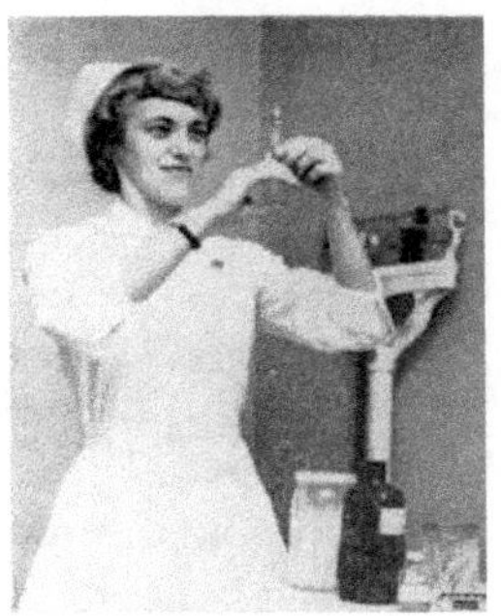

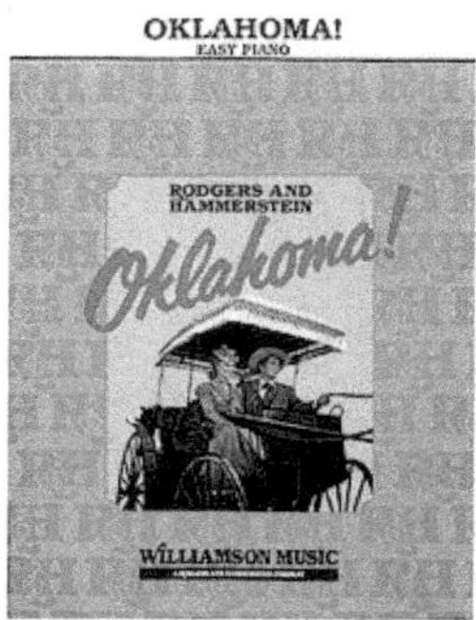

Poster of Oklahoma

Oklahoma Audition

The week following the eventful nurse's visit, I find out that the local theatre group, The Opera and Drama Guild, is going to be holding auditions at Victoria Hall in Cobourg for the musical, *Oklahoma*. Having given up my aspirations of a stage career for marriage and teaching, I'm still drawn like the proverbial moth to a flame this opportunity presents and begin seriously considering that I should audition for the part of Ado Annie. I played this part, to great local acclaim, in a Cobourg Collegiate production eight long years ago. I know I can do it and do it well but I am more than a little concerned. First of all, it will take time from school preparation and being a mom. Second, but more worrisome, is the fact that it is considered a risqué part, and I'm not sure my School Board will approve. I rationalize each concern into oblivion: the Board will only find out after the show is performed; the weekly *Cobourg Sentinel Star* will likely give it no more than a passing nod being more concerned with sports, farm news, and ongoing social teas; as far as performing goes, I already know the songs, and, should be able to quickly learn my lines as memorization comes easily to me. I'd been in a number of plays in high school and feel confident I know exactly what the time commitment will be.

I test the waters by mentioning it, casually, to Rosamonde and Tante as something I've been thinking about. They both think it's a good idea, saying I need something to take my mind off my long hours of school prep and marking. When Jim is home the following weekend, and I ask him, he says I should do it if that's what I want to do. It's a somewhat ambivalent answer, but I decide to take it at face value as encouragement.

For the next week, after Bruce is in bed, I walk around the Manning property and sing Annie's song, "I Cain't Say No." Luckily, I remember all the words and soon begin to feel my old stage confidence returning. I don't realize that being a teacher requires a certain degree of acting, and that this ability is one of the reasons I'm succeeding in my one-room school.

On a Sunday afternoon in mid-October, I show up at the audition, discovering that I am expected to have a song with which to audition. When I tell the director, the charming but formidable Doris Dunlop, that I have played the part of Ado Annie and know the songs, she has the pianist find "I Cain't Say No" and asks me to go up on the stage and sing the piece. I hold my head high and march up onto the stage, refusing to show one iota of my nervousness. Once the opening chords are played, I'm into the song, even managing a few hand gestures and movements as I sing. The assembled hopefuls clap when I finish and I'm fairly sure I aced it.

The following Tuesday evening, Mrs. Dunlop calls to say I have the part. I'm ecstatic and refuse to consider that there might be complications or difficulties. The production will be in mid-April and rehearsals are on Wednesday evenings and Sunday afternoons. Bruce is in bed by seven most evenings and Jim, when he's home, always has to leave right after lunch on Sunday. I can manage this and I will.

During rehearsals that begin in November, I slip into another world, one far removed from teaching obligations and parental duty. For two to three hours twice a week, I become the promiscuous Ado Annie who cain't say no. I love it; thrive on it and have no problem slipping back into a dutiful, responsible wife, mother and teacher on all other days. I even stop worrying about what the Board might think.

I don't say anything to my students and assume that few, if any will come to see the show in April.

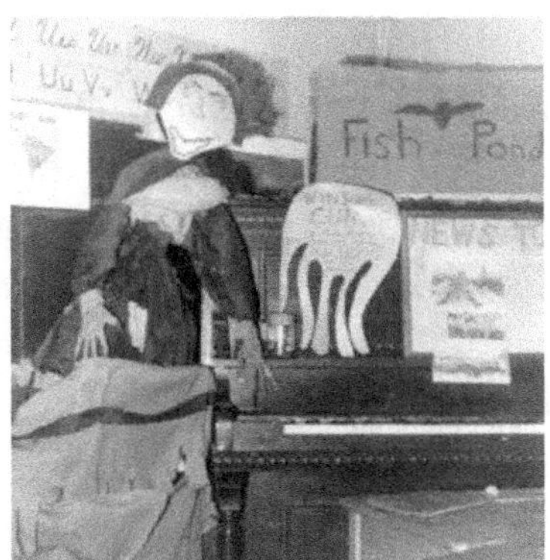

Paper witch in school

The Hallowe'en Party

By mid-October, the children are asking me, almost daily, if we're going to have a Hallowe'en party. One noon hour, I corral my three senior girls to find out what they would expect for this party. They mention decorations, games and, of course, food. The girls say they will ask a number of kids to bring treats and I, impulsively, offer cupcakes. It's probably extravagant of me but I want to do something special for this first party of the school year. I order thirty cupcakes from Andrew's Bakery in Cobourg, specifying that they are to be suitably decorated for my students' Hallowe'en party.

By now, more at ease with my class, I find them to be, for the most part, polite and co-operative. I have loosened my tight discipline rein, and we're beginning to operate more like a large family.

During the morning of Thursday October thirty-first, the excitement is palpable. Before class in the morning, students arrive with covered trays of cookies and sweets which are put on the back table. I have brought two jugs and packages of Freshie. Everyone realizes we have to get through the morning's work, and, other than for junior students reading aloud, the only sound is that of pencils working furiously and the occasional sniffle or cough.

When noon hour finally arrives, lunches are gulped down with much discussion concerning the party surprise my three senior girls are organizing. After everyone finishes eating, and lunch pails are stored under desks, I tell my students to go outside and, unless there is a dire emergency, stay there until called in. Luckily, it's a sunny day.

Susie, Irene and Marilyn remain, one of them retrieving the five-foot step ladder stored in the outer hall, one pulling out the white sheet she has carefully camouflaged in a small suitcase, and one getting out coloured construction paper, scissors and crayons. I help pull the sheet over the ladder, and there is much discussion as to where its preferred location should be. The front east corner is chosen, and we move our "to be" ghost to this spot. Susie makes hands, Marilyn feet, Irene eyes, and I fashion a large "O" mouth.

On the west side, leaning over the piano, they pin up a large leering image of a witch beside a smaller ghost on which is written, *The witch demands a ONE CENT FINE if the teacher catches you talking. Money for the Red Cross.* This doesn't apply during the party but is left up for most of the month of November. We will collect twenty-seven cents.

I clear my desk on which the girls put plates and bowls of candies and cookies. The Freshie is prepared on the back table next to the sink; paper cups are stacked and ready. When I go outside to ring the bell, I find the children already lined up. I do have to tell several of the younger boys to slow down and not push. Once inside, several of the grade-one girls shriek upon seeing the Ghost and have to be coaxed to sit in their desks near the front. Almost, all the rest, flock around the apparition for a better look. Susie, who is behind in getting a bowl of cold, cooked spaghetti ready for "the test," keeps them at bay with an ongoing chant of Boo-ooo, each time drawing out the sound to make it scarier. The party is on!

It's interesting that I don't remember things getting out of hand. Fifteen families and thirty kids. Well, twenty-eight on most days including this party, as the Stoaker children are not here. I'll talk more about them later. Older children keep their younger siblings in line. No one would want a parent to find out that so-and-so was misbehaving at the Hallowe'en party. This is still the era in which discipline is a given. If someone misbehaves at school, it's most likely a sibling will tell and the unfortunate student will be disciplined again at home.

The senior girls organize games, one of which is to be blindfolded and taken behind our splendiferous ghost to have a hand plunged in what the unfortunate victim is told are worms. The cold, cooked spaghetti cut in short pieces is most effective. No one is forced to do this, and some of the little ones shake their heads even before the first person is led in. Shrieks follow, with the victim looking brave and somewhat victorious afterward. The boys often call out how much they like the feeling or try to guess how many worms there are: twenty, a hundred, even a thousand.

I have brought a large cardboard donkey and a number of pin-on tails. They flock around me as I fasten the donkey against a portable bulletin board I have anchored to a chair. When I announce that this is Pin-the-tail-on-the-Donkey and explain the rules, there is much oohing and aahing with almost everyone wanting a turn. I ask the children to form a large circle and hold hands, the two closest to the donkey with a hand on either side of the bulletin board. When I ask for a volunteer to pin the tail on the donkey, there is a decided pause and silence. Finally, Keith puts up his hand and steps forward.

Keith, the self-appointed gag man of the school, is smart and wisecracking, fast on his feet and, seemingly, fearless. As I tie the blindfold at the back of his head, I sense a nervousness I haven't witnessed before. He knows he will likely be laughed at, and will have difficulty finding the donkey, but he's doing it anyway. I now add bravery to his obvious bravado. I turn him around three times, and he veers off in the wrong direction. I have instructed the group to chant "warm" or "cold" as he swerves back and forth, often bumping into the human barrier, causing laughter and loud squeals. After a few minutes, moving appropriately to warm and cold cues, he finds the donkey and plants the tail firmly in the middle of its stomach. He rips off the blindfold and, as roars of laughter follow, throws up his arms, fists clenched, in a gesture of victory. The game goes on longer than I expect as all the seniors and junior boys want to participate, while only one or two junior girls have enough confidence. It's a game of trust and self-exposure, and I note who declines. They need confidence building, especially the girls.

Once four o'clock arrives, almost everyone pitches in to clean up. The younger ones go outside to play while older siblings dismantle the ghost, gather up empty plates and glasses, and put desks back into rows.

After they have all left, I sit in my chair for a while thinking what a wonderful time we all had and how co-operative everyone has been. I am aware of economic differences here, and there is some similarity to the graded schools I visited during my Teachers' College year. It seems to me, however, that here the differences in economic status, learning ability and popularity cause less day-to-day friction, especially during a special event such as this. So far, I have observed that it is more a matter of working to get things done, with older children often stepping in to help younger ones without being asked. The first few times this happens, I am amazed, but as the month continues, I feel it must be part and parcel of being this loosely-knit family. Because I was an only child and lived for many years in isolated country locations, I have no experience with this kind of "give and take." It seems magical to me.

What I fail to see, partly because I am so busy from 7:30 a.m. when I arrive until 4:30 p.m. when I usually leave, is that a certain discrimination dynamic does play itself out in the yard. I never venture out there at recess and noon-hour, never observe the rivalry between siblings and the subtle and not so subtle discrimination between the more affluent and poorer families.

One of my now-adult students tells me that from a socioeconomic point of view, there were two groups of students: those whose parents were economically comfortable farmers and those whose parents were likely labourers, families who rented whatever home in the country they could afford, often from absentee landlords. The *haves* and the *have-nots.* The have-nots were not picked for teams, were left out of games, and ignored, possibly because they were physically inept. I knew they lacked nourishing food and didn't get enough sleep. Too often, as this student bluntly put it, they smelled bad. There would, of course, be reasons: no running water in the house, soap not high on the grocery priority list, parents or parent too tired from long working hours, children left to fend for themselves. I am naive concerning this and too busy getting lessons set and marked to give it a second thought.

I am exhausted for the first month, trying to juggle school during the day and young motherhood early evenings and weekends. I spend at least three or four hours, most evenings, marking and preparing lessons, and another six to eight hours on the weekend. I plunge into this workload with fearless tenacity, and, in spite of the seemingly insurmountable scope of it, I am convinced it will be a good year.

My husband, Jim, is now working at the St Denis Radar Station in the Laurentians, north of Montreal. Every two or three weeks, he leaves the Military Base in Quebec at 5 p.m. on a Friday and arrives in Cobourg around 2 a.m. Saturday. I try not to do school work when he's here, and, on Saturdays, we always do something special with Bruce, who at one-year, seems to accept this as normal. He's always excited to see his Daddy and wistful as we wave goodbye Sunday after lunch. I don't have time to worry over the fact that there is so little time to be together as a family with no privacy. It's our reality, and we make the best of it. This continues for the two years I teach, and, when I think back, during that entire period, as a family, we likely had less than a month together.

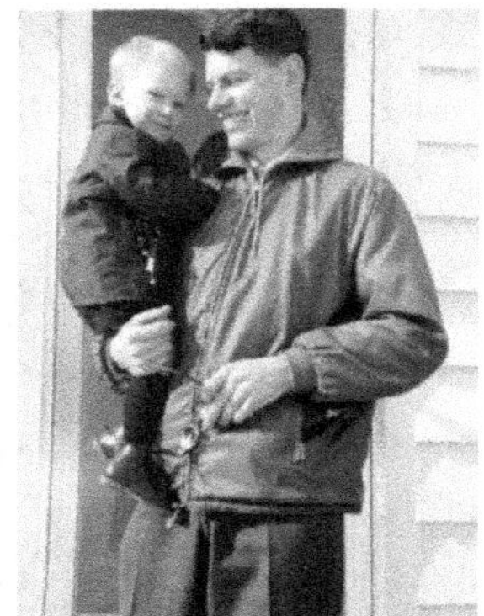

Bruce and Jim

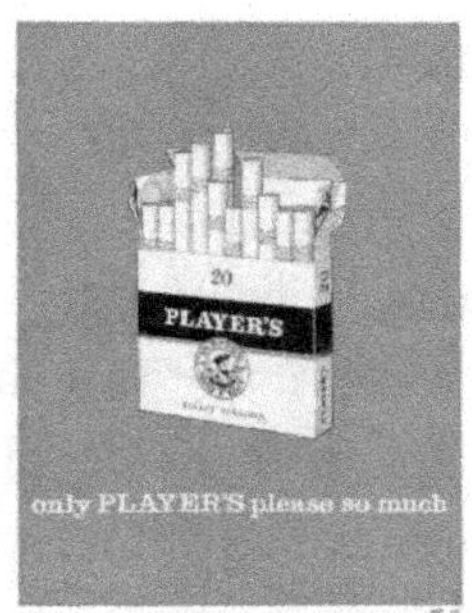

Players cigarette package 1960's

Smoking in the Shed

The Monday after Hallowe'en, I'm pleased to see the Stoakers present and am too busy with lessons that morning to notice sly looks passed between some of the grade-six and seven boys and Gerald Stoaker. Thirteen years old in grade-five, Gerald is the elder Stoaker, nearly six feet in height. He never participates in class discussion and does a minimum of seat work. I know children can leave school at fourteen if they are needed on the farm, and I'm fairly sure this will be Gerald's fate.

As it's unusually warm for the first week of November, everyone hurries outside less than fifteen minutes after beginning lunch. A short time later, a junior boy comes into the school and up to my desk. He looks guilty but, at the same time, obviously has something to tell me. Everyone knows I abhor tattling and that there may be a price to pay in doing so. "Yes?" I say, without looking up a second time.

"They're smokin' in the shed," he says, almost in a whisper.

Alarm bells go off. "Smoking?" I'm already on my feet. "Who is smoking?"

" Gerald and some of the guys."

"In the shed?"

He nods. I'm past him in a flash and nearly to the door. "Thank you for telling me," I say, racing out.

As soon as I appear running full tilt toward the wooden shed, everyone stops whatever they are doing. The yard is in total silence. I stop abruptly and yank the door open. Cigarette smoke pours out.

"What do you think you're doing?" I shout at the top of my lungs, emphasizing each word. "You should be ashamed of yourselves." I stomp inside, hands on my hips. "I can't believe you would do this. It's stupid and dangerous, and you're setting a pathetic example."

At this point, all five boys are hastily butting out their cigarettes into the dirt floor. I've never yelled at any of my students before, but I'm doing it now full force. I'm sure my face is red and I maybe ejecting spittle. I don't care that three of the five boys tower over me. I don't care that it's five against one. At that moment, I'm taller and stronger than all five of them put together.

"Hand over the cigarettes." I hold out my palm. "You'll be sorry if you don't." Gerald steps forward, and plants a partial package of Player's cigarettes in my hand. "Thank you. Now all of you into the school and heads down on your desks."

I follow them, all of us striding in a single row to the front of the school, past the groups of children hushed and watching, up the steps and inside. I open the girls' toilet door, noisily slam the lid up, and hurl the package as hard as I can down into the putrid depths.

They are a sorry bunch, seated heads down on their respective arms, four of them obviously repentant, Gerald rigid, turning his head as I pass, looking almost pleased with himself.

"Sit up," I say, once at my desk. "Let me have a look at you." They sit up, and Gerald continues to look smug. "So you thought you were smart, bringing smokes to school?"

"It was my younger sister what brought them," he says, sticking his chin out.

"And who told her to do that?" I snap back. "Let me guess."

"Won't do it again." He is staring at his desk now.

"And what about the rest of you? I'm sure your parents will want to know about this."

Two of the boys stare down at their desks, and one gives his desk a pound. "Don't," he says, almost in tears. "Give us the strap but don't tell."

"And do you think everyone won't be talking about this?" I come around to the front of my desk. "You'll be the talk of the Front Road School. Five foolish boys smoking in an old wooden shed, a possible fire trap." I look at each one of them, in turn. Even Gerald is beginning to back down, his shoulders slumped, his arms tight against his body.

"I'm not going to strap you," I say slowly, "because if I did, you'd all have bleeding hands. That's what happens when a teacher, who trusts you, is betrayed. No, you'll stay after school today and wash all the blackboards. and tomorrow, after school, the entire school floor."

When I ring the bell, everyone enters in total silence. The windows have been open, and I know every word I said was heard outside. We carry on with the afternoon. At recess, I request that the five stay inside and write me a letter explaining their behaviour. Several of the letters turn out to be quite long and poignant. Gerald's says only, "Sorry Mrs. Manning, from your friend Gerald."

He complains loudly about staying after school saying he has to make sure his sister gets home safely. His half-hearted job of blackboard washing makes it clear he doesn't care, and, once finished, he saunters out in a grandiose manner, taking off at a run once outside school property. He and his sister don't show up again until mid-November, and I wonder whether I should have handled the situation differently. How, I have no idea. I was furious, and righteous indignation knows no bounds.

The following day, everyone continues to be somewhat quieter than usual: fewer pencils sharpened, fewer trips to the washroom, less questioned asked. For a good month following, everyone behaves impeccably, no arguing, no complaining, no pushing in line. I guess they have seen the fury side of me and no one wants to do anything to provoke it again.

By Friday, everyone is at ease again and we're operating like we always do. Once everyone has left that day, I sit at my desk a while wondering what, if anything, did children say to their parents. Probably the less said the better.

By today's standards, it seems almost inconsequential, certainly not worth the fury I rained down on the unfortunate five. But as I've already mentioned, the teacher in the 1960's held great power. With everything else moving at lightning speed, I soon forgot the incident. I'm sure I mentioned it to no one.

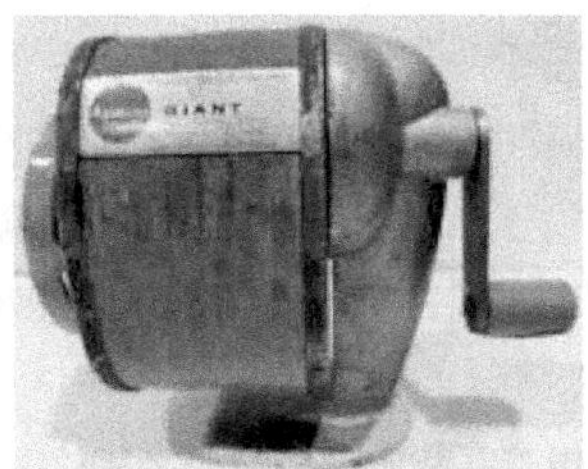

Apsco pencil sharpener

The Pencil Sharpener

By the beginning of November, I am well into the groove. The stove is on now when I arrive in the morning, and I am most grateful. Wood is stacked neatly nearby and the older boys make sure it stays well stoked at all times, as my Board member had mentioned in July. Frost has rendered the outside grassy yard dull beige, ice on the patch of earth at home base most cold mornings.

I am finding the worn-out pencil sharpener a constant irritation. It eats pencils and we are going through the box on hand at an alarming rate. I contact Mr. Moore, my Board member, and say we need a new one. He hems and haws, citing lack of funds and the need to make do. I tell him we are wasting pencils and will likely need another box before Christmas. He still seems reluctant and, in exasperation, I suggest I will pay for a pencil sharpener out of my salary. I add that my students are increasingly frustrated by the old one and that I owe it to them to have it replaced.

The following Monday, a new pencil sharpener is in place. Even before the children come inside, word has spread. A new pencil sharpener! The chatter entering the class increases as they trail in, each one stopping to admire our new acquisition. It's an Apsco, grey with a handle on one side.

Following the Queen and Lord's Prayer, when I ask if anyone would like to sharpen a pencil, the entire class raises its hands. I have the students go up grade by grade with older sibling helpers automatically assisting their younger counterparts. This is serious business with each student admiring his or her newly sharpened pencil, keen to give it a try. Other than for a twenty minute nonstop grinding of the sharpener, the class is admirably quiet. I am pleased for them and think how, in most graded classrooms, the appearance of a new pencil sharper would not be received with such unabashed gratitude.

CURRICULUM	First Period	Second Period	Third Period	Fourth Period
READING — Reads with understanding and appreciation	E	E	E	E
COMPOSITION — Expresses ideas clearly and accurately in written and oral work	E	E	E	E
SPELLING — Spells correctly in written work	E	E	E	E
HANDWRITING — Writes legibly	E	E	E	E
SOCIAL STUDIES — Understands history, geography, human relations, and citizenship in a democracy				
ARITHMETIC — Knows number facts and applies them correctly in problem solving	E	E	E	E
SCIENCE — Expresses interest in science and uses the facts to understand environment	E	E	E	E
ART — Expresses self in creative art	E	E	E	E
MUSIC — Participates in music activities	E	E	E	E
HOME MECHANICS — Knows tools and materials and their use in home tasks				
PHYSICAL EDUCATION — Develops physical skills, including strength, agility, and endurance	E	E	E	E

A check (√) after any of the following items shows a need for improvement. No check indicates performance that is acceptable or better.	First Period	Second Period	Third Period	Fourth Period
SOCIAL HABITS:				
Practices courtesy in speech and action				
Works and plays well with others				
Conforms to school regulations				
Accepts responsibility				
Respects public and private property				
WORK AND STUDY HABITS:				
Comes prepared for work				
Uses careful methods of work				
Completes work on time				
Keeps profitably busy				
Cares for materials and equipment				
HEALTH AND SAFETY HABITS:				
Practices simple health rules				
Observes traffic and other safety rules				

E—EXCELLENT ACHIEVEMENT—is a mark given to the pupil who through industry and effective use of his abilities has produced an exceedingly high quality of work.

G—GOOD PROGRESS—is a mark given to the pupil who has produced a good quality of work.

F—FAIR OR ACCEPTABLE PROGRESS—is a mark given to the pupil who has produced an acceptable quality of work, all factors considered.

U—UNSATISFACTORY—is a mark given to the pupil who through lack of industry, of ineffective use of his abilities, or absence has failed to produce an acceptable quality of work.

2   3

Sample report card

First Set of Exams

Since I have already been told by my students that December will be taken up getting ready for the Christmas Concert, I know I must set, oversee, and mark exams in November. So along with my regular work load, I begin to prepare these. Oral reading can be done within regular class time, as can writing. The spelling mark, I decide, will be an average of the next three regular weekly spelling tests. The rest—grammar & literature, geography & history, math and science—will have to be separate tests for the juniors and seniors. By now, planning to be there for two years, I am following my former teacher Miss Hogg's system of using alternate years to teach history, geography and science. This year, I teach the grade five and seven curricula in these subjects, and in the second year it will be the grade six and eight courses.

We have Art every Friday afternoon, and the mark, I decide, will be for a scrapbook of work put together by each student in grades four to eight. I quickly discover there is no money to buy scrap books, and so we make do by having students punch two holes in each piece of their art work, creating a separate cover, and binding it all together with a provided piece of twine. This works better with some than with others. Even though I explain that the holes must line up from page to page, many do not, and their books become substantially uneven making it difficult to turn pages, even ripping some, much to the consternation of whoever's book it is. When marking, I try to concentrate on the cover design and its neatness rather than on the challenge of book binding.

After the first music class in November, I tell Mr. Thrip that I am handing out Report Cards Monday, November 25th and will need his music marks the week prior. He says he gives letter grades and will have them ready for me. I am hoping our added weekly music sessions will result in better marks.

For me, setting that first set of exams turns out to be a steep learning curve. On Friday November 1st, I announce to the class that exams and tests will begin the week of November 18th and run for four days. Even though I have mentioned, beginning in late September, that this would be the case, there is a round of groans silently amplified by grim faces, especially from the seniors. I promise I will post a schedule on Monday. This means I must *have* an exam schedule. It turns out to be a long working weekend with very little sleep. My mother-in-law, Rosamonde and her sister, Tante, are more than generous with their time, keeping Bruce occupied as much as possible, cooking meals and looking after me as though I were a daughter. I will be forever grateful to both of them.

The next two weeks become a time-scramble, with me making sure I set exams as well as carry on with regular classes. I already know that most of my students dislike history, continually groaning over my ongoing detailed questions posted on the blackboard. Science fares a little better, although when going over answers with each grade it's easy to see who has not read or barely read the text. When marking the exams, it's not infrequent to find an answer that bears no connection to the given question.

Overall, my exam questions turn out to be much too difficult, especially in history and science with a number of my senior students failing one or both of these exams. Enough, that I feel I must apply a bell curve to prop up the marks to a decent standard. I am fairly sure not many parents are familiar with a bell curve so I add a class participation component and lower the mark percentage for each exam. This turns out to be a win-win solution. Students are pleased their marks have gone up, parents are pleased their children have been participating well, and I am relieved the marks don't make me look like a second-rate teacher.

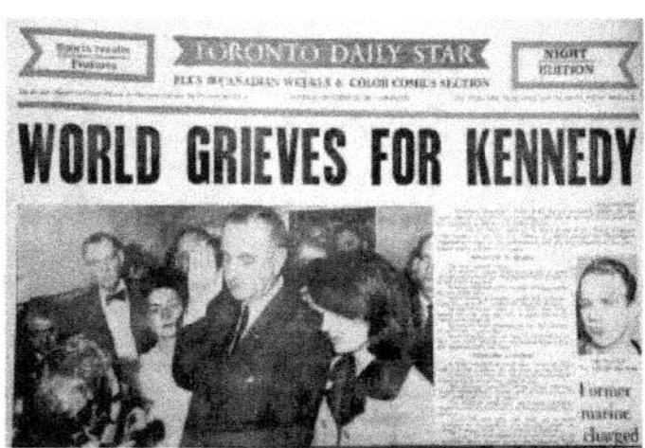

Newspaper clipping of Kennedy assassination

Assassination

The day following our last exam turns out to be a date many will always remember. American news has not been a front-line interest for most of my students, nor for me, that year. I am too absorbed in lesson preparation, marking, and the general well-being of my school. Friday, November 22nd is a rare exception, one that consumes most of the class for the afternoon and well into the following week. It is, of course, the assassination of John F. Kennedy, the charismatic President of the United States.

This news is discovered initially by my senior girls who, at noon hour, while marking workbooks for me, turn on the radio expecting to hear their favourite Beatles music. Instead, they find a minute by minute update of the president's death with descriptions of the Dallas motorcade, Jackie Kennedy holding her dying husband in her arms, voice soundtracks of the chaos, bystanders' screams, police sirens, and general mayhem. All workbook marking stops. The girls, in tears, retreat outside. Within minutes, the usual noon hour playground chatter and noise grind to a halt. When I ring the bell, a sombre procession enters the school, the little ones confused as to what has happened, but looking as serious as their older siblings. Once seated, Marilyn comes to my desk and asks if the radio can be turned back on.

We listen for over an hour, a rerun of the actual event first, Kennedy being pronounced dead in the Parkland Hospital's Trauma Room, and, as it is happening, Lee Harvey Oswald killing a police officer and being subsequently arrested in a movie theatre.

The older girls keep sniffling which sets off the younger ones, most of whom do not fully understand. Even the boys are quiet, a number of them looking grim-faced. When a grade-one boy stands up and asks if the bad guys are going to storm our school and will we get killed too, I realize I must explain the logistics of distance relating to this situation.

I turn off the radio and pull down the map of Canada and the US so I can locate Dallas, Texas. When another primary student says tearfully that it doesn't look very far, I ask Joe Harper, who is good in math, to find the distance scale on the map and figure out the mileage from Cobourg to Dallas. When Joe works out that it's almost 1500 miles and would take, at least, five days to get there in a car, a number of the younger students look relieved. I realize how little they understand of relative distance, most of them never having travelled further than Cobourg two miles east, or Port Hope three to the west. I momentarily think how exciting it would be to create a course around this topic, part math, part geography, part social history.

Instead, I read to them, three more chapters of our new-to-them novel, *Treasure Island.* Young Jim and his mother have just unlocked the sea chest, finding some money and a map showing an island where great treasure may be buried. The district squire buys a ship, and Jim becomes its cabin boy. Tension and excitement mount, and, when I close the book a few minutes before the end of the school day, there are groans and pleadings to read more. I smile as I remind them the school day is over and it's time to go home.

They leave, many still talking about what it would be like to be Jim, to go on a schooner in search of adventure. Only my trusty three senior girls who stay to clean the boards and brushes begin talking again about Kennedy and the real trauma of the day.

The following Monday, there is renewed talk of the event, increased in intensity by Jack Ruby murdering Lee Harvey Oswald while being escorted by police to the Dallas jail. I tell the children that this is history-in-the-making and that these events will end up in history books for their children and grandchildren.

We already have a Current Events bulletin board but to date I am the one who has brought in most articles. It's time to formally add this to our curriculum, and I ask for volunteers to bring newspaper clippings and report on interesting Canadian and world events. What I discover is that most students' households do not get a newspaper, and of the few that do, *The Cobourg Sentinel Star* is their paper. Marilyn and Nancy say their families get the weekend *Toronto Star* and *Star Weekly*, and, if the paper doesn't get used in the stove, each one promises she will bring it in on Mondays. After a month goes by and no one has brought in any reported news—nothing about the Vietnam War or the Civil Rights movement in the States—I stop asking whether anyone has a current event to share. A number of families have TV's, but I have to assume no one talks about news events. Current history slides back to its former minor position. I am too busy with the day-to-day pressures of teaching to give it any priority.

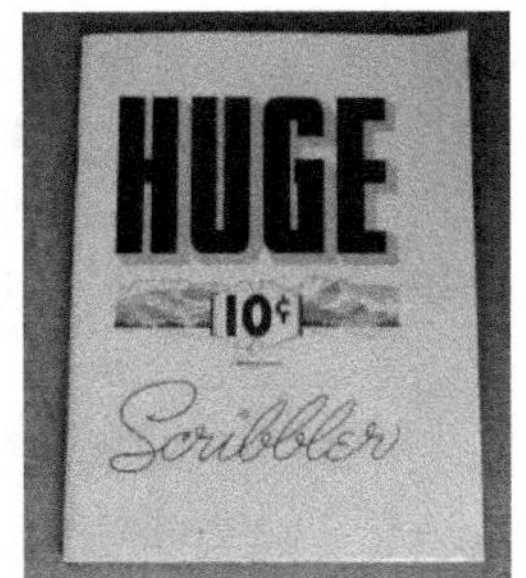

Scribbler used in the 1960's

Open House

As soon as exams are over, we plunge into getting the room ready for the evening of November 28th Open House. On the Friday following exams, for most of the day, we work decorating the six big windows. Grades one and two share a window, while each of the other grades has a window to themselves. Since each window has eight panes, there is more or less, a pane for each child to decorate.

At this point, I feel I must say something about the Stoaker children. They are poorer than any of the others, walking to school in all-weather with no hats, mitts or socks. The two of them show up the first day of school, and from then on attend only occasionally, in the end, completing less than one third of the school year. Their mother comes to the school once, not for Open House, but a few days before. She is neatly dressed in a worn-thin skirt and jacket and apologizes for her children's lack of attendance, saying they are needed to help at home. Two of her front teeth are missing and her hair is overly windblown having obviously walked the three miles to the school. I have no social worker qualifications or experience with anyone like this and remember being sympathetic and feeling totally inadequate given the circumstances. The most difficult part of dealing with these children—Gerald age thirteen in grade five and Essie ten in grade two—is that they rarely wash, and smell quite foul. So much so, that they are ostracized at recess and noon hour, and, other than for racing around at games lacking body proximity, everyone avoids being too close. This is not possible in the classroom, and their empty desks most of the time are a relief not only to those sitting close, but, I have to admit, to me as well.

When present, they are polite but distant, Gerald, especially, simply biding his time until he turns fourteen the following year and can leave. They don't come for exams or Open House or attend any of our special events. So, even though I have thirty students on paper, from day to day, I have only twenty-eight. That I mention it now may seem trivial, but it does mean, from a decorating point of view, there will be enough window panes for every student.

While many students cut pictures out of magazines, a few juniors and seniors create their own art, some of it quite spectacular. We quickly discover that the magazine pictures need to be mounted on construction paper otherwise they are rendered unrecognizable by what shows through from the opposite side. This extra step of gluing proves to be a challenge for some of the grade-one students especially Kim who cries profusely when she is caught eating the white paste instead of applying it on her picture.

Over the weekend, I make a grade name tag for each window. I place them beginning on the south-west side with the "Grade One" sign and moving clockwise around to the east side ending with "Grade Seven." The following Monday morning, everyone comments on the windows, and at noon hour, almost every student walks from window to window looking at and remarking on the work of other grades.

For the Open House evening, I tell each child to pick the workbook they feel demonstrates their best work. For the rest of the week, everyone manages to finish his or her work early and there is a fair amount of time spent rubbing out and redoing or adding illustrations to scribbler covers. By the time Thursday afternoon arrives, each student is pushing to make everything as perfect as possible. When a student asks to wash the top of his or her desk, then they all insist it must be done. The little ones spill more water than they use and older siblings step in to scold and wipe up puddles. As well, during afternoon recess, several of the older students offer to clean and wash all the blackboards.

Even though our regular story time is Friday afternoon, I decide that Thursday following afternoon recess, to continue reading *Treasure Island.* We always do a recap of what happened in the previous week's chapter, and I'm always impressed by how much many of my students remember.

The boat has set sail now and, although the plot continues to be too advanced for the little ones, they sit quietly listening. I love reading aloud and, give as much life to Jim, Long John Silver, and Captain Smollett as I can. At the end of each chapter, I ask questions about the characters and what they're up to. The answers are often more insightful than I anticipate and frequently incredibly funny, especially from the little ones.

As soon as everyone leaves that afternoon, I inspect the room, tucking in errant items hanging from desks and setting each notebook straight. I'm nervous about this first Open House, having no idea how many parents will show up and what they will expect from me. Last week, I sent home a note, handwritten with copies mimeographed, saying that I would be happy to answer any question or comments they might have. The event is to begin at seven with me welcoming everyone and inviting my students to show parents their desk, work, and the window displays, after which refreshments will be served, and I will wait to see if any questions follow.

I've ordered five dozen assorted cookies from Andrew's Bakery and pick them up on the way home. Instant coffee, tea bags and hot chocolate are already in place at the back; a kettle and paper cups I will bring. I briefly considered asking my Board member for a kettle but decide, so soon after the new pencil sharpener, it would not be politically wise. My senior girls have offered to take turns serving drinks and, as with the Hallowe'en party, I will put the cookies on my desk, this time beside the open attendance book and the bell.

I arrive home late and spend some time with Bruce while supper is being prepared. He is not happy when I mention I will be leaving again shortly after six. Lucky for me, he is easily distracted by dear Tante who often plays peek-a-boo games with him. After supper, I race upstairs to change my clothes and manage to slip out the door unnoticed.

It's a good thing I'm there early as parents and children begin arriving well before seven. Someone has miraculously stoked the fire so that it crackles and gives the room a cozy air. I put the kettle on to boil on one of the hotplate burners, and it's already bubbling by the time the door first opens.

Most children are dressed in their good clothes, some of the older boys sporting ties and white shirts. It's like a cocktail party without alcohol and I'm so wound up, I probably chat too much, trying to interact with each set of parents. As I suspect, it's mainly the parents of children who are doing well who have come to see me. They sound pleased with my teaching, and a number mention how much their children are enjoying school this year. This is in part due to the fact that the previous teacher was apparently overly strict and, I gather, somewhat unforgiving. From everyone's point of view, I have come bouncing in, much younger and filled with new ideas.

Years later, one of my students told me they all thought I was about sixteen when I started at the school! I was sure they knew I was married and had a small son not that would prove I wasn't in my teens. I felt I was immeasurably mature and responsible and it never occurred to me students or parents would think me not an adult. The board members knew but, obviously they didn't deem it necessary to say anything.

Some of the Board members have come to the Open House and mainly they stand, hats in hand, looking mildly uncomfortable, while the women and children chat and move about the room. Still unsure of how well I am doing as a teacher, I begin to surmise from the parents' comments and compliments, that I am coping admirably. This a huge relief to me, and I think I may have relaxed just a little. I am acutely aware, however, that I am "the teacher" and that in this position I must balance appropriately between being the one in charge and being friendly. No one asks me any difficult curriculum or discipline questions and they chat mainly about the weather, about what's going on in the community, and about my photo in the *Star Weekly*. Several parents do ask about a Christmas concert, and I assure them there will be one.

By nine o'clock, everyone but a couple of my senior girls and their parents is gone. They help me clean up, and, as the last one to leave, I lock the school door and pause to look first about the school yard then up and down the deserted highway stretching in both directions. I haven't been here after dark, and the somewhat decrepit wire fence structure behind the baseball diamond produces an eerie shadow against the frozen ground. On most schooldays, many are still playing baseball and will, I guess, until snow covers the ground. I am still bursting with conversations, my students' obvious excitement, and more parental approval than I dreamed of.

As soon as I arrive home, however, every part of my body feels weighted down. Rosamonde has hot chocolate ready and wants to know how everything went. I begin telling her but keep yawning, and, as soon as my mug is empty, she strongly advises I make my way to bed.

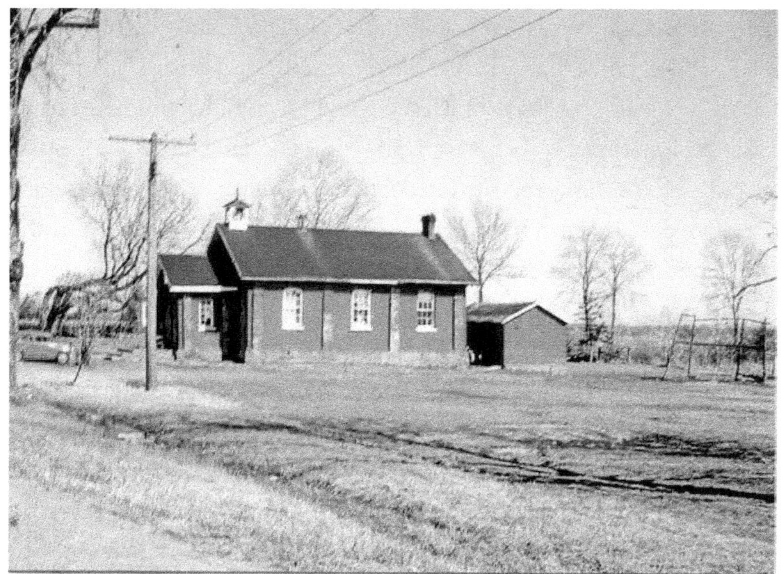

The School

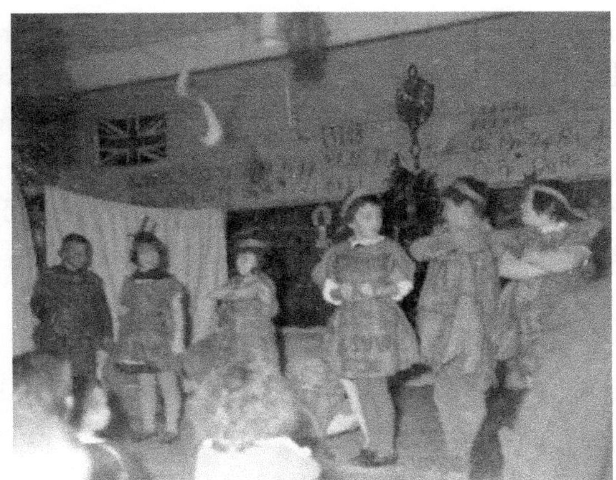

Christmas Concert

Christmas Concert 1963

As the last school day before the holidays is Friday December 20th, I decide the Christmas Concert will be that evening. I originally determined it should be the day before the last day but then rationalize that, as nothing useful will be done that Friday, it might as well be a bang-up end to the first term. By this time, I'm getting used to making time-line decisions. Students never question, and I have no one to ask.

On the Monday afternoon following Open House, we spend an hour discussing the logistics of this concert. I discover there is a portable stage platform in the shed. The senior boys will bring its sections in when requested. When I ask what we will do with my desk, I am told it will be moved to one side of the stage and that the hooks up high on the opposite walls are for a curtained back stage area. I have never noticed the large metal hooks eight feet up, and am told that when they are connected by a line and strung with curtains they will cut off the south west corner. A senior girl mentions that the teacher before me provided old brocade drapery curtains, but she was sure we could make do with sheets. Another student points out that a second rope is to be strung along the front of the stage for the curtains and connected to another hook on the west wall. When I look a little dismayed, two of the senior girls say they will bring enough sheets to do the job. They assure me that the existing hems in these sheets will work to thread a rope through. One of the boys says there are two long pieces of rope in the storage cupboard at the back and, striding back there, produces them for me to see. I have been so busy preparing classes and marking, I have never looked in this cupboard.

The most pressing question is when to put up the stage. The seniors want it up right away, citing it will be easier to rehearse on the real stage. I decide to wait until the week before our concert as I sense having the platforms in place will raise anticipation to a fever pitch, and we do have lessons to get through in the meantime. I relent, however, to having my desk moved on an angle to the west side of the room. By pushing the front desks back a couple of feet we have created a rehearsal and set-making area.

The next task, in my spare time, is to create content for this concert. Trying not to panic, I ask the children to make program suggestions. "The juniors do a play," someone says, "and the seniors act out the Nativity with a student reading the Bible story." They also mention junior and senior chorus pieces and a quartet which they are already practising with Thrip. I have barely noticed this, always being so busy marking when he is there. To this list, they add story-reading, carols and, of course, Santa and presents. We only have three weeks and time is of the essence.

Taking a deep breath, I promise I will have a program in place by the end of the week and, tomorrow, will ask individual volunteers to put their name on the activity list that I will put on the board.

This week, after music classes, Mr. Thrip tells me, rather apologetically, that he will not be able to attend our concert as he has been informed of one of his town school's concerts being on the same date. He hopes I can find a parent or older student to play the carols, and, as he has only one copy of the choral pieces he is sure they will work being sung a capella. I think I said we would have the best Christmas Concert ever, but as I was close to tears, I don't remember.

Photocopying, as we know it today, was nonexistent in the 1960's, especially in smaller Boards of Education. I remember from my student teacher days in Toronto that any photocopying was done by the school secretary who kept the machine in her office, locked. As a student teacher, with no priority, I was only able to photocopy seat work endorsed by the teacher to whose room I was assigned. Usually, this teacher said it was better for me to write whatever was needed on the blackboard. I knew this had a double purpose, that of assessing my blackboard writing skills as well as the content I would be teaching.

Although I am too upset to ask, it is most likely that Mr. Thrip cannot photocopy music. It wouldn't be a problem as long as he is playing the pieces to be performed in any school. If I had known about this situation, I might have asked him which dates would work for him but being so preoccupied with my own schedule I didn't think to find out.

That evening, much to my young son's displeasure, I begin organizing the concert before supper. Sitting at a small table in the front room instead of at my usual hideaway upstairs in the bedroom, I pretend to play Fisher Price garage with him while making a tentative list that will become the program order. He keeps leaning on me, grabbing my knees and saying, "Mama" over and over. With each interruption I bend down and move a Fisher Price person one way or the other, saying something vaguely appropriate, at the same time working on my list. Children know when you're not giving them your full attention, and his knee pestering increases until I give up with the list and sit on the floor with him.

At supper, feeling increasingly out of my depth, I bring my list to the table. When Rosamonde asks if everything is all right, I almost burst into tears. "I'm working on the Christmas Concert," I say, feeling my throat constrict, "and I don't know what I'll do about an accompanist."

Tante, whose sensitivity radar is always on, smiles and nods. "I would be pleased to play for your school concert," she says. "What would it entail?"

"Three choral pieces," I begin, wondering how in the world she could do this on such short notice and read from my list. "Two choruses, a quartet made up of senior girls and Christmas carols."

Tante smiles her gracious smile. "I can use a hymn book for most of the carols. And I assume you will have music for the chorus pieces and the quartet."

"I'm looking into it." I'm aware it's an outright lie. I thought naively if I asked Mr. Thrip again, the music might magically be available.

"Well then," Tante adds, smiling. "It's as good as done."

I must admit, at this point, I really know very little about Tante. She's the unmarried aunt, now sixty-eight years old who has always lived with the Manning family. Being a mere twenty-three at the time, I think of her as an old woman. She plays piano beautifully and I have been told she graduated from Toronto Conservatory as a concert pianist but never worked professionally. She quietly helps run the household with her widowed sister Rosamonde, and I remember her toiling over the ironing board, ironing sheets and pillow cases to perfection. She loves cats and birds which often proves to be a conflict, as she places pans of water out on the lawn providing free game for the two house cats. Years ago, she wrote stories for her nephew and niece, Jim and Jacqui, who remember wonderful tales of two donkeys: Skeegee and Loto. Tante has also laboured for as long as I have been living there, on both a biblical play and old-testament epic novel. I remember her reading passages of it to me. She also writes poetry and paints. A devout United Church member, she is known for the elaborate and stylish hats she makes to wear on Sundays. She is a Renaissance woman whose talents are never widely realized and whose love of family emanates from her like a soft halo. That she would offer to play for our Christmas Concert without seeing the music ahead of time is a testimony to her talent and the way she lives her life.

I tell Tante, that I'll get the music for her, if at all possible. I feel, momentarily, like Pinocchio, but squelch my lie by smiling reassuringly at her. She still plays the Steinway parlour grand in the Manning living room; not as often as she used to, Rosamonde tells me, as arthritis in her hands is now a problem.

Finding a suitable play for the junior children seems impossible until I find an older set of readers containing a play called "The Zoo" inside one of the tall, glass-doored bookcases. It's poorly written and quite ridiculous but entails using an unnamed number of children as zoo animals, and so fits the bill. There is a narrator, and the action merely follows the storyline with a few main characters having speaking lines. My theatre-self hates it but my more practical teacher-self knows it's the best we can do. Parents gladly pitch in to make costumes and several of my artistically-clever students create the sets.

The Nativity set is more straightforward as bales of straw are readily available, and someone brings in a white wicker basket for the crèche. There is much snickering when I read out parts, especially those of Mary and Joseph. I hush the children with one of my dastardly looks, and we carry on. I have seen enough Nativities over the years to be able to make up the stage blocking (Appendix 3) as we work on it the first time through. If I veer off the expected course, someone speaks up to say that isn't the way they are used to doing it. Most of the time, I agree.

The week before the concert, when Mr. Thrip arrives to go through the three choruses and the quartet, I'm pleased to tell him that Genevieve Groulx has agreed to be our accompanist but that she has asked about music for the choruses. "And you told her," Mr. Thrip says, "that I have only this copy and the children will sing their pieces unaccompanied." I nod, still hoping, I guess, that some music miracle will occur and there will be extra copies. The children, bless their hearts, don't seem the least fazed and, when Mr. Thrip has them sing their pieces unaccompanied, they perform reasonably well. Whatever will I tell Tante?

That evening, I am so upset, I can barely eat my dinner, and my son, sensing his mother's distress, becomes cranky and difficult.

I wait until I've tucked Bruce in bed, rushing through his bedtime story, and not being a particularly patient Mom. I find Tante in the kitchen carefully drying the dishes, humming quietly to herself. She stops when I enter and puts down the towel, looking at me quizzically. "Something is bothering you," she says softly.

"There is no sheet music," I blurt out in a rush, feeling tears near the surface. "Mr. Thrip, the music teacher, has only has the one copy and it's not for us."

Tante puts her hand on my arm. "Not to worry," she says. "I will play by ear."

"But. . ."

"They are Christmas pieces, are they not?"

I nod.

"It won't be a problem." She gives me a hug. "Don't be upset. It will all work out."

On the Friday before the concert, I put all the children's names in a paper bag, and each draws out the name of the person for whom they will buy a gift. We have decided it must cost twenty cents or less. There is the usual groaning and smiling as each child discovers whose name they have drawn.

After much soul-searching and discussion with several of my older students, I do not include the names of my two rarely-at-school Stoaker students. They have not been present since mid-November and have no parts in any of the Christmas concert. I feel badly and wish there was something I could do.

In the late fall, after talking to my board member, I had driven to their run down farmhouse and paid a visit. Their mother, who was outside hanging some grey stained sheets on the line, met me at the road, and it was obvious I was not to be invited in. The house, if it could be called that, was a sort-of ramshackle house trailer, patched with rusted tin in a number of places. Two younger siblings were sitting in the dirt playing with sticks.

"I know my kids doesn't make it to school all the time," she began, "but there's so much work to do here on the farm with their Dad away and all. I need them to help me with chores."

I nodded, not knowing what to say.

"Ger'll be fourteen in the new year so he'll be leaving school to tend the farm full time."

"I see," I said, feeling more and more out of my depth. What could I say? There was nothing, at this point, I could do to help. I held out my hand. "It's been good meeting you," I said, and knowing I sounded as phony as a single, well-employed, middle-class young woman would to her, added, "Hopefully, Gerald and Essie can make it to school soon." She nodded and went back to the clothesline.

Once at my car, I looked toward the barn. The roof sagged and there was an enormous pile of manure close enough to give off its pungent smell. I couldn't see any livestock and imagined they were out in the field beyond.

The Stoakers did show up a couple more times before the weather turned cold and so, now, I have to hope they won't turn up at the concert. Two days before the event, still worrying about them, I go to the Chainway Store in Cobourg and buy two pairs of mitts. Wrapping them and tucking them under the tree appeases my guilt. My sensible self knows there is nothing I can do while my emotional self, always wrestling to be dominant, wants to help somehow. As always in my life, it's a great divide I am unable to close.

A week before the concert, after lunch, the senior boys gather round my desk to tell me that each year they go to woods beyond the school property to cut a Christmas tree. When I ask whose property it is on and will this person mind, the boys assure me it's not a problem.

"Shouldn't I ask the board?" I query.

They all shake their heads, and someone says they have been doing it for years. Today is the day, they tell me, as one produces an axe while another waves a rope in the air. To haul it back, they tell me. Needless to say, I feel pressured but with six pairs of young male eyes staring at me, several of them stomping with impatience. I think about it, only briefly and then give in.

They reappear after everyone else is back inside, working on lessons. There's a buzz as they haul the tree inside, propping it up against the farthest south-east window.

One of them disappears out the door again and another reassures me he is going to get the pail and bricks needed to set the tree in. When I ask about decorations, a senior girl goes to that same back cupboard I have never inspected and pulls out a battered cardboard box. She and another girl drag it to the front and open it. One pulls out a ragged star and the other some well-worn strings of tinsel.

Once the tree is secured in the pail and water poured in, I say, "Enough. We will decorate the tree tomorrow." The rest of the afternoon is only moderately successful from a teaching point of view.

The next morning, almost everyone arrives with a tree decoration. I haven't asked for this and am somewhat amazed. "We always do this, Mrs. Manning," is the reply when I ask. "Much appreciated," I manage to say. I am so proud of these children.

During the week of the concert, we do a "run through" each afternoon: the plays, the readings, the choruses and the quartet, with me using my pitch pipe to get each musical piece started. I assure them that Miss Groulx—I print her name on the board and pronounce it, "Miss Grew"— will be playing the piano for their pieces as well as the carols.

"But how will she know our pieces?" one girl asks.

"She can play by ear and will be able to follow whatever you are singing."

They are impressed, several uttering ahh's and nodding. I am not at all sure they know what "playing by ear" means, but as I have told them it will work, they believe me.

It strikes me at that moment what a position of power I hold. Whatever I say, they believe. I am the authority. They know, however, when it comes to spelling, I am not the authority. I told them back in September that spelling was not my strong point, and that if I made a spelling mistake on the board, someone was to tell me. It didn't happen often, and when it did, whoever told me would come up to my desk and whisper, looking somewhat embarrassed. I always thanked them and corrected the error.

What I didn't know then and found out only when I attended university in the 1970's, was that I am dyslexic. I had always done poorly in math and spelling from grade school in the 1940's to high school in the 1950's. I would be told I wasn't being careful enough or I hadn't studied enough. Until I graduated from grade thirteen in 1959, laziness, sloppiness, and carelessness were common responses to my mistakes. This made me nervous during tests which only increased my wrong answers.

The amazing fact is that dyslexia was discovered in the late 1800's. It was not until after the mid-twentieth century, however, that dyslexia, as a reason for student errors, was widely identified in schools. As a mature student at university, it gave me such a feeling of validation to know there was a reason for my mistakes other than a deliberate lack of trying. Now, of course, my computer automatically switches letters when I type them the wrong way around. I watch it, amazed and thankful.

The day before the Christmas concert, everyone lugs in their costumes. Changing back and forth, drastically increases the time taken between pieces, especially when the set has to be changed as well.

However, between afternoon recess and four o'clock, we do manage to make our way through the entire program. We do another run through the day of, and it goes more smoothly. The last hour before dismissal is spent moving desks to the back and bringing all chairs available into rows, with the front row less than three feet from the stage. Junior desks are pushed to each side, with occupants often complaining that whoever is moving their desk is too rough as things keep falling onto the floor and need to be retrieved. Once all seats and desks are in place, the chaos subsides and everyone looks pleased and expectant. It will obviously be one of the most exciting evenings of the school year.

I arrive home to be unexpectedly greeted by my husband, Jim. He has managed to get enough time off to make the five-hour drive home from Quebec and be here for supper before the concert. Overjoyed, Bruce is racing back and forth shouting, "Da da, Da da," at the top of his lungs. Even though I am incredibly nervous about the evening ahead, it is a celebratory meal indeed.

After supper, while I'm getting ready, fussing over what I will wear and going through a last minute list of things that might be needed that evening, Jim reads to our son and helps Rosamonde get him ready for bed.

We agree that I will be dropped off at the school first and Jim will return closer to show time with Tante. When we pull into the space in front of the school, well before seven o'clock, light snow covers the entire yard and a half moon creates a picturesque black and white landscape. The cement steps and stoop have been recently swept by the ever efficient Mrs. Carr, I imagine. I never see her at work, and met her for the first time at Open House. She keeps everything in pristine condition: the floor, sink, desks, even the toilets which are always clean, equipped and smelling of powdered lye. I must remember to thank her after the concert.

By the time Jim arrives with his aunt, the room is half-full. She makes her way to the piano and promptly begins playing carols quietly. I continue to be amazed by her blasé attitude, seemingly un-rattled that she has no music for any of the required pieces. As I recall, for each piece, I would sound my pitch pipe giving the starting note and she would respond with the complementing chord.

Once everyone piles in, with wet boots stuck under the side desks and coats piled on top, my little school is in a proverbial "bursting at the seams" state. The fire has been more than amply stoked and the temperature hovers around eighty degrees Fahrenheit. Fathers loosen ties, and many cheeks are glowing. Parents, mostly mothers and siblings, fill the assembled chairs, many of the adults with legs too long. Fathers and older brothers lean against desks or stand at the back. Grades one to four sit as tight as sardines on the floor between the front seats and the stage, while grades five to eight perch against desks along either side.

As soon as I stand on stage, there is an instant quiet with only a few preschool visitors whispering and chair-scraping. I introduce myself, welcome everyone, and the show is on.

The program is fairly straightforward and by today's standards, unbelievably simplistic. The energy, however, is the same as with any school performance: each participant wanting to do his or her best, some more confident than others, a few displaying showmanship beyond their years. Stories, choruses, instrumental numbers, the Nativity, a turkey draw, Santa, presents, and food.

I remember the "Ten Little Indians" presentation. No teacher would think of having students perform this skit today. It was used widely, at the time, and even though the sentiment is neutral, I do find it a bit shocking to think I used it with so little concern.

The grade one and two students, involved, are so excited to be wearing costumes and proud to recite their numbers one to ten in front of an audience. I suppose today it could be puppy dogs or porcupines! If you don't remember or know the sequence, here is the politically incorrect version:

One little, two little, three little Indians

Four little, five little, six little Indians
Seven little, eight little, nine little Indians
Ten little Indian boys.

The children stand in a row and sing/shout the number they are, ducking down and up as they do so. Once up to ten, the process is reversed back down to one. Now when I look at it, the last line "Ten little Indian boys" is not only racist, but also sexist! Neither of these politically charged terms was heard of in small town vernacular at the time.

I have some not-so-great black and white photos: one of the Nativity, one of Ten Little Indians, and one of the play called The Zoo. Someone is on his hands and knees, and has an oval shaped piece of cardboard with spikes coming out of it that look suspiciously like pencils strapped to his back. There is obviously a confrontation going on, as some other unidentified creature is close by. Whatever it is, and whatever happens, it is greeted ultimately with thunderous applause and cheering. Enthusiasm completely overshadows any lack of sophistication on all levels.

One of my students now tells me it must have been her Dad who came in as Santa. Whatever his excuse for not attending the concert was reasonable and definitely not to be questioned at the time. She said it was only years later at a family get-together, that the secret was revealed.

I am incredibly nervous and distressed when a few things go wrong. The sheet curtains do not pull back and forth easily, and, by the last act, the rope holding them is sagging substantially, rendering pulling an increasingly difficult task. Some students forget lines, and the prompter is often too loud, which always causes a ripple of laughter through the audience. My cheeks redden, and I wish we had practised more. However, each scene proceeds smoothly, and given our limited resources and venue, we put on a good show.

Soon after the concert, everyone flocks around Miss Groulx, and a number of children give her gifts. Several musically knowledgeable adults comment on her ability to play by ear. She smiles and thanks each one, and then she and Jim slip quietly out. Being four decades older than I am, she must be exhausted.

After much jovial conversation, eating and back-patting, families begin to leave. Little ones are getting cranky, it being long past their bedtime. My few faithful senior girls and their mothers stay to help me clean up. We take down the curtains and pack up the Christmas tree ornaments. Many have been already taken by those who brought them; the rest go into the battered cardboard box. Mrs. Carr assures me she will come to clean the floor, now strewn with crumbs and crumpled serviettes, as well as put the desks back in order. I am so tired I don't protest even though I know it will be a major job.

With the last person gone, I put on my coat and turn off the lights. A moon has risen and light floods in from the large east windows giving everything in the room a surreal, dramatic appearance. Long shadows stretch from desks, chairs, even the crumpled serviettes—the overall effect is a black and white collage. It's a set, my set, the best I could do, and as adrenalin diminishes, I slump into a chair letting my head rest against the wall, waiting for Jim to return. My first semester is over. I know my students now, the relatively well-off farm kids and poorer families who rent less desirable dwellings in the country. Fifteen families, thirty kids.

My eye catches the two pairs of mitts still under the tree. I retrieve them and decide I will present them to the Stoaker children when they appear at school next. I vow to make 1964 even better than the four months just past. I have new ideas, new projects to begin, things that will improve this little front road school.

I don't hear the door open and jolt upright when Jim taps me on the shoulder. He pulls me to my feet, telling me again, what a great job I have done. I nod, and am asleep as soon as the car pulls out onto the highway.

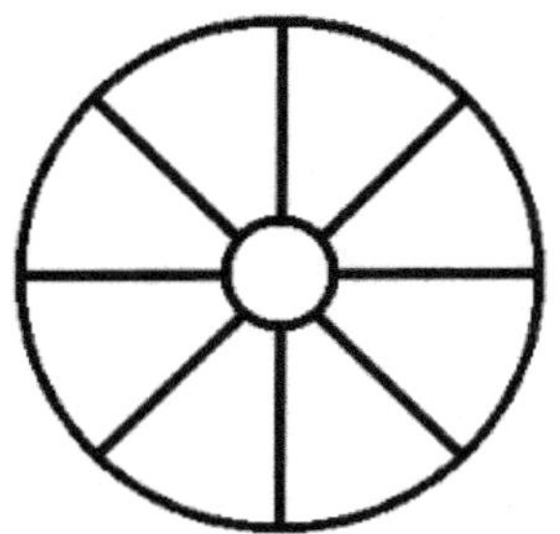

Fox and geese snow pattern

Snow Games and Mitts

January 1964 brings snow and rain and more snow, all of it cold and miserable. It's dark when I scrape snow and ice from my car early each school morning and often dark when I leave the school for home. However, the weather does not deter my students from boisterous outdoor recess and noon-hour play. Daily freedom from our somewhat smelly, crowded one-room is greeted with enthusiasm three times each day. Only heavy rain or sleet will stop them from piling on coats and mitts and venturing out into the fresh air.

The older children make a spoked wheel pattern in the snow for a game they call fox and geese. It always creates much squealing and chatter through the windows at recess and noon-hour (Appendix 4).

I wish now that I had taken more time to watch the children play this game. The first few times their squeals reach fever pitch, I venture to the window to see the wheel pattern beaten down in the snow with two or three children crowded together in its centre. Someone else is chasing a classmate up and down the paths joining the inner circle with its outer periphery. When caught, that person does the chasing. I only watch a few minutes, being immersed either in marking workbooks or in preparing lessons.

Those who walk to school often arrive wet and chilled. Mitts, hats and even coats are draped on chairs close to the wood stove, the room quickly smelling of wet wool combined with a medley of household smells. As the wind usually gusts from either east or west, snow accumulates on respective window sills, and those sitting close to these windows often move their desks closer to the stove. Everyone wears heavy sweaters and many put snow pants back on once they are dry.

The Stoakers show up for one day early in January. I have saved the mitts, and I note, as the two of them remove their thin, badly-patched coats, that they have no mitts. I'm anxious to give them their post-Christmas presents. As I have had no luck communicating with Gerald since the smoking incident, I decide I will give the mitts to Essie who is three years younger. I wait until noon hour and quietly stop her before she goes outside.

"These are your Christmas presents," I say, handing her the two wrapped packages. "Since you weren't here for the concert, I saved them for you."

"Thanks," she says, not looking at me. "I'll put them with my brother's coat."

The afternoon proceeds as usual, and I have almost forgotten about the mitts, other than hoping they will put them on to go home. After I announce dismissal and almost everyone has left, Gerald appears with the two packages in his hands.

"I'm givin' these back to you," he says, shoving them onto my desk. "We don't wants them."

"But they were Christmas gifts," I say, and lying, "I don't even know who they're from."

"Don't take charity," Gerald says glowering at me and, turning abruptly, stomps from the building.

I'm so furious I can barely contain myself, almost as full of fury as I was when I found him smoking. How could he deprive his younger sister of warm mitts? Who was he to say what she should or shouldn't have? Charity? No, it was common sense, kindness, something to make their difficult lives less so.

I don't remember what I did with the mitts. I certainly couldn't use them. What I didn't understand was that this family, as poor and lacking in almost everything most people took for granted, had one thing that couldn't be taken away from them—and that was their pride. They didn't show up, again, until early spring, and I did notice they were wearing gloves, worn ones with holes in the fingers, but gloves that were their own.

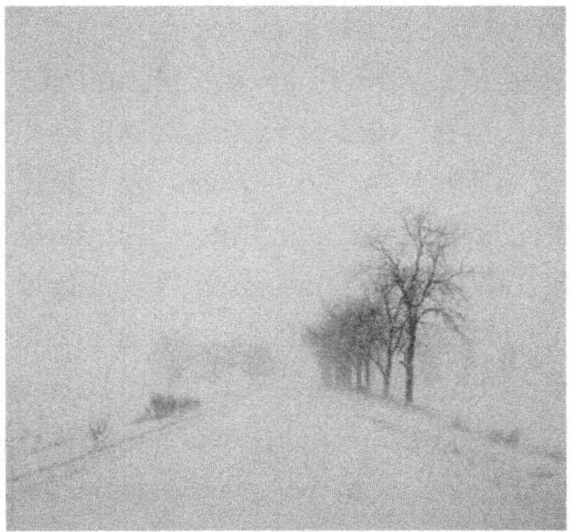

Snowy road

Highway Accident

It seems that this month of January is full of unpleasant surprises and the week after the mitt incident, I am faced with a situation substantially more serious and traumatic.

Here, I digress with some School Board jurisdiction background. Two of my students, Kim and Trevor Barton are one of several families who, before this school year, attended a Cobourg school. In 1963, municipal rules changed and those not living on town property were required to attend a school closest to where they lived. These families had town property or, in the case of the Burnham family, these parents had donated property for the town to build Cobourg's Burnham School. This new ruling meant that children who previously attended graded classroom Cobourg schools were now required to come to my one-room school. I know the parents of these children were not, initially, happy with this and I'm sure it was a shock for students formerly in a graded classroom to face our modest set up.

I have never heard any complaints though, and a month or two into the school year, I hear by word of mouth, as it is in a small town, that both parents and children are pleased with my teaching. I know I'm enthusiastic and dedicated and, after only a few weeks teaching, these children have become part of my family. The fact that I, alone, am responsible for their well-being and education is a daunting task that, at twenty-three, my youthful-self embraces with no hesitation. Growing up as an only child, living far from any relatives, these children have quickly become my own, their lives and hopes always within my radar.

On a snowy afternoon near the end of January everyone, except a couple of the senior girls who are helping with marking, has bundled up and set off for home. About ten minutes later, a senior boy races in yelling, "Kim's been hit. Kim's been hit." I grab my coat and race outside, my two helpers close behind. It's snowing and visibility is not good. A short distance down the road, a car has stopped. Trevor stands, fists clenched, beside his fallen sister, while an adult, most likely the unfortunate car driver, bends over her snowsuit clad form.

"She darted right out in front of us," a woman says, in halting tones. "My husband has gone to that house (she points to the Moore's across from the school) to call an ambulance."

"I thought she was right beside me," Trevor says, his young voice breaking. "She said she was crossing with me." He pounds his fists against his legs and tears spill down his cheeks. "She wouldn't take my hand."

I squat down beside Kim, flat out on her back, eyes closed, face stark white. "Kim," I say. "It's your teacher, Mrs. Manning. Can you hear me?"

Her eyes flutter open briefly. "I got hit," she says weakly. "And it hurts."

"You mustn't move," I say, putting my hand lightly on her forehead. "You're going to be fine. A doctor is going to make you better."

"Kim's cold," she says, staring up at me now. "Will the doctor make me warm?"

I pull off my coat and cover her with it. There's a brisk wind but I don't feel it. My dear little Kim. Hopefully, only bones are broken. My two senior helpers, Irene and Susie, are beside me, and Susie pulls off her coat. "Here," she says, "use mine too." I tuck part of it under Kim's head. She almost smiles, then closes her eyes again, tears slowly running down her cheeks. I pull a Kleenex from my skirt pocket and wipe them away, fearing they will freeze on her face. "Kim's cold," she whispers again. "I want mommy."

"We know the parents," the woman says, "and my husband said he'd call Kim's mother after he gets through to the ambulance. Lord, I hope it doesn't take too long."

Both girls are shivering now, standing beside me, arms wrapped around their slender bodies. "Go back," I say to them. "You can watch from the window." They wait only a few moments before turning and running back toward the school. I notice how careful they are to check for traffic before crossing to the school.

The husband appears and I notice they're both quite young, perhaps not that much older than I am. I can't imagine hitting a child. His face says it all. Regret, fear, concern. "I'm the teacher," I offer. "Mrs. Manning."

"I saw the boy," he says somewhat shrilly. "But she came out of nowhere. Right in front of me." He squats down beside me. "The ambulance is on its way and I've called her mother. She should be here in a few minutes."

We hear the ambulance before we see its lights tunnelling through the snow. I stand up feeling stiff and suddenly cold. Very cold. Everything goes into high speed after this. Two ambulance attendants jump from the vehicle and pull out a back board and a stretcher. They slide the board under Kim who only whimpers briefly, then lift her onto the stretcher. I retrieve my coat and Susie's. A police car pulls up and the man and woman disappear into its back seat to be interviewed. Just as I'm about to tell, one of the ambulance drivers who I am, Mrs. Barton pulls up in her car. Trevor flings himself into the front seat as she bolts out from the other side. She races to the ambulance as they are sliding the stretcher inside.

"Kim, my little Kim," she manages before breaking into tears.

"Mommy," I hear Kim call, her loudest voice yet. "Mommy, I'm cold."

There's a brief discussion between Mrs. Barton and the ambulance driver and then the two vehicles are off, the ambulance with its siren full blast.

I've pulled my coat back on although I don't remember doing so. When I arrive at the school, Irene and Susie have made me a cup of tea. I can't stop shaking and, although I know it's not just because I'm cold, I tell the girls that's the reason. Their faces reflect the shock and fear I feel. All we can do now is hope Kim is not too injured and that everything will right itself. One second, I think, that's all it takes. In one second, cause and effect drastically alter reality. Before and after. Then and now. "Poor Trevor," I say to the girls, "it's awful for him as well as Kim."

"And Mr. and Mrs. Barton," Irene adds, pouring more hot tea to my half-filled cup.

Two days later, we find out that Kim has a broken shoulder and leg. She will be in hospital for at least a month. It frustrates me that I cannot visit her. Visiting hours, at the Cobourg General Hospital, are from two to four in the afternoon, family members only.

Several days after the accident, I go to Kresge's to look for something I can give the child. In the toy aisle, I'm immediately drawn to Gumby and Pokey. These two bendable rubber-like characters, the green human-like Gumby and the orange and black horse Pokey started as a clay animation cartoon series in the early 1950's. By the sixties, both the TV series and the spin-off popular toys have become staples in many family households. Whimsical and capricious on the screen, they appeal both to adults and children. I find them delightful and have already bought a set for Bruce. I impulsively decide they are perfect for Kim and buy them, hoping she doesn't already have these toys.

The next day, Trevor confirms she has no Gumby or Pokey, and after school, I stop in at the Barton's to drop them off. Trevor is nowhere in sight, and Mrs. Barton, still looking worried and drawn, stays at the open door. She says Kim is doing as well as can be expected. She smiles somewhat weakly and adds her little daughter asks each day if she can come home and cries when her mother leaves. Her voice has a lovely Scottish burr to it, and I commiserate with her about the limited visiting hours at the hospital. I leave feeling bereft all over again and wish there was something more I could do.

Each day after school, now, I pull on my coat and mitts and hurry to the outside door in order to wait and watch as the children walk down the highway, some crossing to the other side. Everyone is careful and, after a week of enduring wind and snow, even sleet a couple of times, several older students tell me not to worry, that everyone looks out for the little ones, and so I abandon my after-school watch.

Since the accident, Trevor is quieter, often asking to stay in at recess to read, or, he says, to study. I go along with this the first week after the accident, realizing he doesn't want to be pestered for details and reruns, but on the second Monday I insist he go outside with the others. I quietly ask a couple of the older trustworthy boys to keep tabs on him and make sure no one is questioning him. It takes a few more days, but gradually he returns to being himself again, his smile returning more often. I purposely don't ask him how his sister is, but the following Monday, he lags behind at recess to tell me he and Kim played a Gumby and Pokey game when he visited her on the weekend.

January disappears into February, and still Kim is not back. I have been sending home work for her to do—simple printing and a reader that I hope a family member will listen to her as she tries to read. When I ask Trevor how she's doing with it, he just shakes his head and looks the other way. This doesn't bode well for her as she will be so behind.

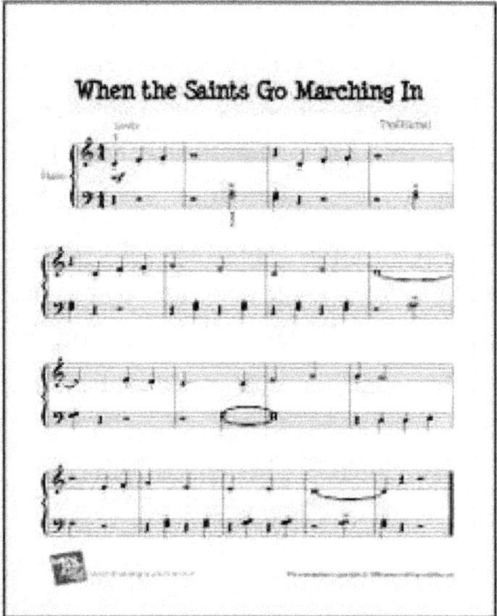

Sheet music "When the Saints…"

Rhythm Marching

Early in February, Mr. Thrip tells me he is concerned that so many of the younger children are unable to keep time and that he has decided to try rhythm marching as a way to improve this. He suggests we could move desks so that the children can march around the periphery of the room. Grade three students Paul, Wayne and Trevor help me and there follows a noisy dragging of desks with pencils and belongings falling onto the floor.

Then, as he suggests, I line the children up at the back of the room, and he begins to play a loud marching tune with an accentuated rhythm. The children look at me mystified and no one moves. I step to the front, beckon them to follow, and begin marching, swinging my arms in time. Most of the older children catch on, while the younger and less confident ones either run to catch up, or wander along stopping to pick up fallen items, or, in the case of one or two, back themselves against the outside wall refusing to move. After one lap, I take the wall-clingers' hands and try to encourage them to step in time. A few unsuccessful steps later, one trips, and the other tells me she has to go to the washroom. Meanwhile, Mr. Thrip continues to pound out a Sousa-like rhythm, calling out "Left, right, left, right" in a loud, encouraging voice. When he turns his head and sees that some of the children are definitely not catching on, he stops and says firmly, "That's enough for now. Everyone back in their seats." This entails putting all the desks back, during which time students who can't yet access their seats continue marching, running, and generally causing pandemonium. I stamp my foot finally and demand quiet.

Mr. Thrip now asks the children to stand beside their desks and clap out the rhythm as he plays. Older students, who find this exercise easy, clap enthusiastically and spontaneously begin marching on the spot; the laggards copy as best they can. When he notices several of the grade ones are not clapping, he stops and threatens that if they don't clap properly with the group they will be required to stand in front of the class and perform by themselves. This reduces one to tears, and I try to help. Thankfully, a few minutes later, he checks his watch and announces the lesson is over. I can see he feels frustrated, and I tell him we will work on improving rhythm. I feel he is expecting too much but I'm certainly not in a position to say so.

After the seniors have had their session and everyone is back in, I tell the children we will work on clapping with some of the older students.

We work at it every day, singing simple, rhythmic songs they already know. As well, at recess and noon-hour, a couple of the senior girls play rhythm games with the young ones outside. I teach them a song-game I was already playing with my young son.

Three times round went the jolly jolly ship

Three times around went she

Three times round went the jolly jolly ship

'Till she sank to the bottom of the sea.

I then suggest that one or two senior girls make a snow circle and have the Juniors march inside it, singing and clapping until the last line, when they all fall down with much squealing and laughter. The anticipation of being able to collapse on the last line, seems to help most of them master a reasonable rhythmic proximity. The day before the music teacher's next appearance, I'm feeling fairly confident. And I assume, so are the children.

The following week, however, the two most un-rhythmic students, both girls in grade-one, are absent from school on music day. Singing and clapping go reasonably well, and Mr. Thrip doesn't notice that these two little girls are missing. The following day, they both appear with notes saying they had severe stomach aches in the morning and were kept home.

To say I find this situation difficult is an understatement, but I also know I can do nothing about it. I am aware that Mr. Thrip, likely in his fifties, sees me as a first year novice, and that he is trying to make the best of teaching his music program in my one room school.

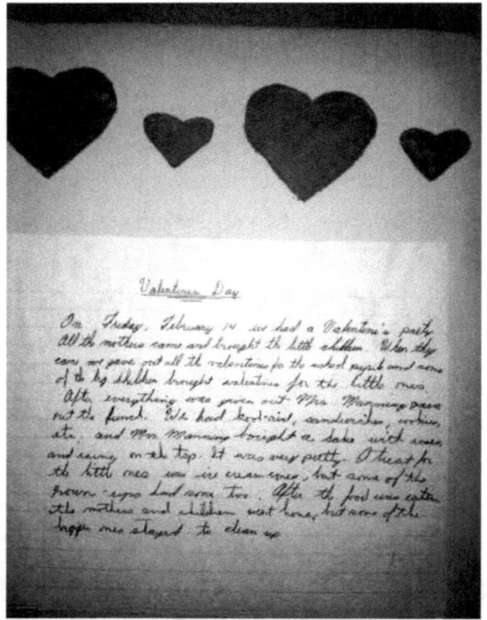

Page from scrap book Valentine's party

Valentine's Party

From the first day of February, excitement is building in anticipation of the annual Valentine's Party. I've been told well in advance that it occurs on a Friday afternoon and that parents and preschoolers are invited. As luck will have it, Valentine's Day falls on a Friday. A week prior to this, I put all students' names into a small cardboard box which I close and shake it vigorously. Then one by one, beginning with the seniors, students draw names to give valentines to. I have dithered over whether or not to add the two Stoaker children's names. Since they haven't been to school since that fateful day in January, I rationalize that it's unlikely they will appear February 14th. I also know that the groaning will increase exponentially from the students who draw their names. I will bring extra valentines and, if they show up, I'll add them at the last minute. As the names are drawn, there is much whispering and tittering, the idea being that the valentine is to be given unsigned, perhaps with or without a clue as to the giver. Older siblings help their younger counterparts, often keeping the names so they won't get lost.

On Friday, from Andrew's Bakery, I bring a large white cake decorated with swirly pink icing embedded with decorative roses, as well as instant coffee and tea for the adults. I place the cake box on my desk and say it will not be opened until the afternoon.

The senior girls bring packets of Freshie which they mix in our two large jugs during lunch hour. The party is to begin at two, which means parents and children will begin to arrive at one-thirty. I know there is no use trying to do lessons after lunch, and so we have a longer noon hour. I am hoping the children will run off some of their pre party energy. The minute the first car drives up at 1:20 p.m., however, they line up and begin coming in, as excited as they were before the Christmas concert.

At this point, I suddenly realize there will be no valentines for the preschoolers. I whisper this to Susie just before we begin, and she says not to worry it's been taken care of. After the students take their seats, several with a squirming younger sibling on their knee, I call Mrs. Carr to the front. Before asking her to begin dipping her hand into the box holding the valentines, I thank her for all her good work in looking after our school and to her sons for providing us with an ongoing supply of wood. A hearty round of applause follows, with several hoots and whistles from the older boys.

She smiles as she draws out each name and the recipient hurries to take his or her valentine. As requested, there are no signatures inside, but a comment which may or may not reveal the sender. There is much whispering and sharing, the grade ones and preschoolers, new to this event, delighted to be receiving a valentine, several of them squealing and racing to a parent to have it read.

Mrs. Carr calls me to the front and hands me a large store-bought valentine in a bright red envelope. Everyone stops talking and all eyes are on me. I open it slowly, feeling suddenly embarrassed, and read the verse inside. All my students have signed the card, even the grade ones, and it's one of those Kodak moments that doesn't get recorded.

Conversation resumes and, when its volume increases to the deafening point, I impulsively whack my desk with a book and announce that cake and drinks will now be served.

A couple of the senior girls rush to the back to give out glasses of Freshie and to mix and pour coffee and tea. Most children line up for drinks first while a few cluster around my desk waiting for the cake unveiling. There is a round of oohs and aahs when I do. Even though it's a large cake, I'm careful to cut fairly small pieces.

To my surprise, John and Keith Wilson appear from the back with two cartons of ice cream and a package of cones. "Little kids first," Keith announces loudly, flourishing an ice cream scoop. Another lineup quickly forms, and after the younger children have their cones and there's still ice cream left, a number of the adults follow suit. There is much chattering and spilling of cake crumbs, with a couple of cones splatting to the floor followed by tears and dismay. Someone grabs the dustpan to scoop up the ice cream, and the tearful child quickly receives another.

By 3:30 p.m. most of the food is gone, and parents bundle up their youngsters, preparing to leave. I dismiss the class, but, as with other gatherings, senior students who walk to and from school, stay to help clean up. Mrs. Carr says not to worry about the sticky floor, that she will give it a wash that evening.

There's a small piece of cake left, and I decide to take it home to my son. He has adjusted fairly well to me leaving every morning and is always watching at a front window for me to return home. Being a working mom is more difficult than I anticipated, and leaving him each day always leaves a part of me wishing I didn't have this job. Bringing home a treat for him once in a while, not only pleases him, it also lessens my guilt. Rosamonde and Tante, take such good care of him, but there's always that voice in the back of my mind that says I'm neglecting my duty as a mother. Tonight, I decide to leave any marking I should do and spend all my time with him, playing and reading stories until bedtime.

It's been another eventful week at the Front Road School and, on Monday, we'll have to get back to regular classes, deadlines, and whatever excitement or challenge next comes along.

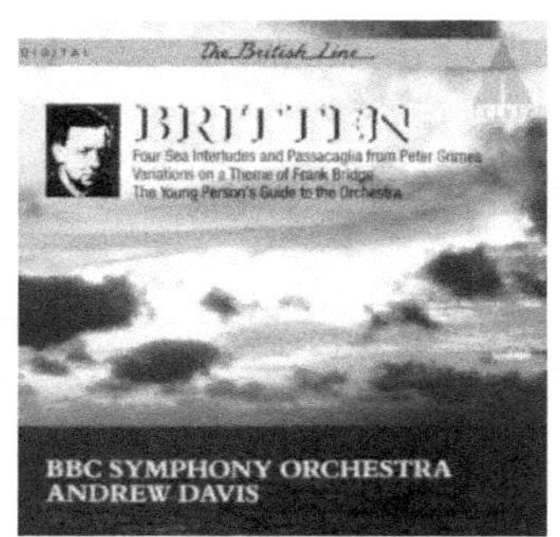

LP jacket Britten BBC Orchestra

Music Appreciation

When Mr. Thrip arrives the first week in March, he announces that today will be a Music Appreciation class. He requests two of the senior boys to bring the record player from his car. I notice a decided look of resignation on a number of the older students' faces.

"You may put your heads down, if you wish," he says, taking a vinyl record from its case, "We're going to listen to *a Young Person's Guide to the Orchestra*. I think I remember that we have at least two musicians here." He pauses. There are a few uncomfortable moments of silence and then Keith and John put up their hands half-heartedly. "Ah yes," he says, looking pleased. "And you play?"

"Trumpet," John says, staring at his desk.

"Trombone," Keith adds, fidgeting with his hands.

"Excellent," Mr. Thrip says. "Anyone else?"

"Cathy Burnham accompanies us on the piano every morning," I say. "There may be others who are taking piano lessons."

Mr. Thrip nods. "I simply want you to listen and enjoy," he says. "This recording tells the story of all the instruments in the orchestra."

"Will you be testing the children on this information?" I ask, thinking I'd better take notes if he is.

"No, no," he says, smiling. "It's music appreciation, something to enjoy. If the children learn from it, or are inspired to try an instrument themselves, all the better." He lifts the needle arm and pauses. "We'll listen to Side One today," he says. "It takes approximately a half hour." He smiles and carefully places the needle onto the LP. The orchestra begins to play.

I have never heard this recording and find it most educational. When I was in Teachers' College, the music teacher there assumed we were all familiar with instruments of the orchestra and tested us on them after only one brief listen to samples of each. Since there were thirteen different instruments, most of which I was hearing for the first time, I could only identify a few. This recording would have been incredibly helpful to me and likely to a number of my student colleagues.

My students, many of whom have little or no musical background, are soon fidgeting and yawning and trying to sit still. At the end of side one, that has highlighted the woodwinds and strings, Mr. Thrip lifts the needle. "We'll stop here," he says, "and listen to the brass and percussion next week."

For some time after the two week music appreciation experience, I keep wondering what I can do to bring some more diverse music into my student's lives, something other than classical music which only one or two know anything about. Rosamonde, Tante and I always watch the Sunday evening Ed Sullivan Show that often features singers and musicians.

After school one Thursday, when Marilyn and Susie have stayed to help me mark, I ask them if they've ever seen The Ed Sullivan Show. They roll their eyes saying their parents watch it, but they don't bother.

"We're usually doing homework on Sunday nights," Marilyn says.

They get giggly at this point, whispering to each other and I suspect they are about to tell me something they consider off limits. "We do watch a TV show after school," Marilyn confides, "usually on Fridays."

She looks at Susie, who continues. "The little store and garage down the road." She gestures west. "Nick and Ethel's." I'm not aware there even is a store west of the school.

"We get salt water taffy or jelly babies," Marilyn continues, "and Ethel always begs us to stay and watch *As the World Turns.* Do you know it?" I nod remembering that Rosamonde has mentioned Tante watches this soap opera almost every day.

"I'm never home soon enough," I add.

"They have a twenty-four-inch RCA," Marilyn says, rolling her eyes. "It's divine."

"Bigger than ours at home," Susie adds.

"We don't want anyone to know, though," Marilyn continues, looking a little worried. "Ethel lets us watch but she wouldn't want everyone piling in."

"I won't tell a soul, I promise."

We return to our marking, and again I wonder how I could bring some more contemporary music into my school. My helpers and I get a regular dose of the Beatles at noon hour but there is no other music available that might be interesting to my students.. On the way home, I suddenly remember that we have a record player and records stored somewhere in the house.

Jim had a Spartan record player when we married, along with a collection of jazz and classical records. When he bought it, the player was mono and played only 78's, one record at a time. He put in a Garrard changer that also plays the smaller 45's and larger 33 1/3 vinyl records. The changer allows a stack of five records that should drop one at a time onto the turntable. However, due to slippage between the records, the sound quality lessens with each subsequent disc loaded, and we know that three records are the maximum number in order to get a decent sound. I recall that the player looks like a bulky brown suitcase, opening with a hinged lid, and that there are built-in speakers behind a metal grill under the changer.

Luckily, Jim will be home this weekend. He makes the 300-mile drive from Morin Heights, Quebec to Cobourg, leaving after work at five, a good six-hour drive on a number of unpaved roads and I'm always relieved to hear our 1962 Austin's wheels crunch to a stop on the gravel driveway, usually around 2 a.m. He's home Saturday but must leave Sunday after lunch in order to get back to the Air Force Base at a decent time. Caught up in the excitement of seeing him again, and giving as much time as possible to activities for the three of us, I forget to ask about the record player until lunch on Sunday. Jim says he thinks it's somewhere in the back of our bedroom closet and says it's fine if I want to share his records with my class.

As soon as he leaves, I tell Rosamonde that after Bruce's nap the two of us are going to look for it. Bruce's small bedroom is off ours and has old walls with no soundproofing; it's out of the question to rummage around in the closet when silence is needed for his nap.

When we first moved back to this house, hauling all our worldly belongings in an eight foot by ten foot trailer behind our car, Rosamonde insisted we take the master bedroom, with the adjacent small room, that was Jim's bedroom growing up, for Bruce. Years of assorted boxes, clothes and other paraphernalia fill the back of this closet but there is ample room for our clothes, household boxes and, thankfully, the now sought-after record player.

Always bright-eyed and full of beans when he first wakes up, Bruce vehemently shakes his head when I ask him if he wants to come into the closet with me. "No, no, no," he says, plunking himself on the floor. I realize that its dark interior with shadows of hanging clothes is too scary. Instead, he jiggles and pushes boxes as I pull them out. I know his interest will soon wane and so I open a box containing our set of Melmac dishes. He squeals with delight, pulling out the daisy-flowered plates and bowls, banging each one on the floor before lining them up around him. Their plastic durability was one of the reasons we purchased the set once we knew we'd be regularly on the move for several years.

Luckily, before he becomes bored with the dishes, I find the record player and a box containing our modest record collection. Momentarily, nostalgia kicks in as I remember our basement apartment in Kamloops, BC and listening to Moe Koffman play "The Swinging Shepherd Blues." I will definitely take this LP to school, as well as *Canada's Story in Song*, a two album set by Canadian folk singer, Allan Mills and a few others that might interest my students.

Looking at the array of dishes now scattered in all directions, I quickly decide to leave both the record player and box in the closet until Bruce is in bed.

Trying to convince a one-and-half-year old to put the dishes back into a box is considerably more challenging than asking my students to do something. "No," he says each time I ask, and when I put a dish back, he promptly pulls it out again. He only agrees when I suggest we take the filled box downstairs to show Grandma.

On Monday, I bring the record player to school and set it up. It's open on my desk when several of the early arrivers come in to warm their hands at the stove. By the time I step out to ring the morning bell, there is a buzz up and down the assembled line. Before opening exercises, hands shoot up wanting an explanation.

"It's my record player," I say. "I brought it so you could listen to some new music." There are a couple of groans, and I add, "Only with special permission at noon hour. If you try a record and don't like it, try another." I leave it at that and begin the day. That noon hour, when Marilyn and Susie come in to mark books, they ask if they can play a record instead of listening to the radio. They choose the Moe Koffman Quartet LP, and I show them how to carefully place both the record and the needle. Once it's playing, we return to marking and, after a few selections, Marilyn politely asks if we could switch to the radio. Given these two girls listen to more music than most of my students, I have a feeling that I will have to come up with something more than just listening if I am going to interest the whole group in these records.

The following noon hour, however, Keith and John come in asking if they can listen to a record and request the same Moe Koffman LP. At the Christmas concert, they played a duet, trombone and trumpet respectively. When I ask why this LP, they tell me that Susie said it was some guy playing a musical instrument.

"He plays a flute and, sometimes, a saxophone," I say. "Not the instruments you boys play."

"That's okay," Keith says, taking a second look at the cover, "My uncle told me he used to play sax." They listen to the entire LP, albeit chatting for a good part of the time. As the girls aren't needed for marking that day, there's no conflict.

The wonderful thing about a one-room school is, because of its shabbiness and lack of physical amenities, anything brought into the environment is deemed exotic and subsequently sought after. So it was with my record player and records. John and Keith created a following, even Susie and Marilyn, and I designated two noon-hours a week for what became The Music Club. Initially, I restricted the group to grades five to eight but after Cathy Burnham kept asking me daily for a week why she, who played the piano and was familiar with classical music, was not allowed, I opened it up to anyone who was interested. Both Keith and John quickly caught on to running the machine and they taught several of the others as well. Initially nervous they might scratch our records, I soon realized they were probably more careful than I was.

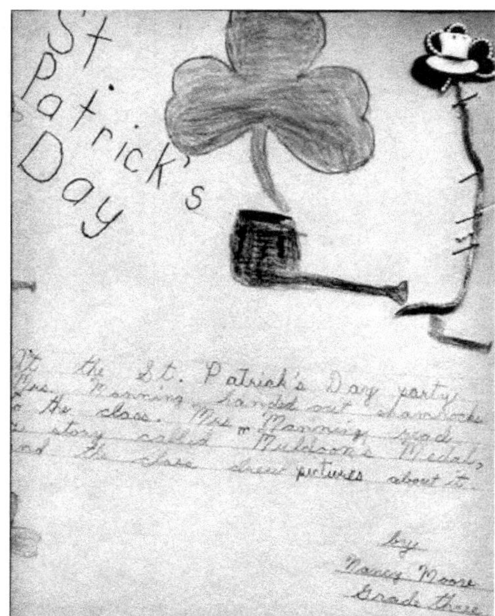

Page from scrap book St Patrick's Day

Spring and St Patrick's Day

By mid-March, most snow is gone but, even though the school yard is soggy and wet, everyone goes out both at recess and noon hour. The girls have begun skipping on the poured cement slab between the highway and the school steps. The grassy area alongside the school where I parked in the fall is still too soft for parking, so I angle my car onto one side, leaving enough room for double-dutch.

Unknown to me, a group of older boys regularly trek to the edge of the far west field where higher ground makes a more acceptable playground. Someone has come up with the ingenious idea of making forts. To facilitate this, they have gone across the fence into the adjacent farmer's field and "borrowed" a number of slats from the long line of snow fence put there, annually, by Provincial highway maintenance crews. By carefully pressing these upright slats into the thawing ground and weaving long grass in and out between them, they form a wall, just far enough from the page wire fence so that a roof, the distance of a slat length, joins the wall to the existing fence. Once grass is woven in and out on this roof, a perfect fort exists. Apparently, there are several of these forts far enough from the school, all undetected in the drab, early spring landscape. This enterprise, involving trial and error combined with perseverance, continues into April, and, by the time more long grass has built up in front, these forts are well camouflaged.

I knew nothing about this until I began interviewing my now-well-into-middle-age students. Paul Burnham told me they were incredibly popular and that likely no one said anything about them because of stealing the snow fence slats. "We knew you wouldn't approve," he added, grinning. No one was ever late when I rang the bell and I don't recall seeing anyone running toward the school so perhaps someone had a wrist watch or, more likely, a designated student who remained near the school at recess, checked the time inside and signalled the others when it was time to return.

At the beginning of March, a number of comments or, rather, hints are made about a St. Patrick's Day party as well as an Easter party. March 17th falls on a Tuesday, and, given our current work load leading up to Easter exams a week away, this request for two parties before Easter holidays seems a little excessive. However, I promise something special for the afternoon of March 17th. The Monday before, I purchase, at Kresge's, thirty small cloth-embossed shamrocks. Each one has three heart-shaped petals edged with small white beads, a jaunty white plastic top hat trimmed with green, glued on top. Attached to each shamrock is a long white pipe cleaner stem.

While everyone is outside at noon hour, I place one shamrock on each student's desk, not sure what their reaction will be. Once coats and rubber boots are off, the new acquisitions are inspected, and from the oohs and ahhs, I gather, appreciated. I announce that I am reading them a St. Patrick's Day story and that they can draw an illustration when it's over. It is difficult to find a suitable story and, this one is from an old reader on the top shelf of our never-used library. "Muldoon's Medal" is sentimental and not particularly well-written but the class seems to enjoy it. Students' illustrations vary from shamrocks and pipes to interesting versions of Muldoon, some as a younger man and some looking more like a green-clad Santa. I promise to post their drawings on the back wall which is our current Art Centre.

Once everyone is ready to leave, I remind them to take their shamrocks home, knowing from experience that several younger ones will likely forget, and when, the following day, they still can't find them, tears and frustration will follow.

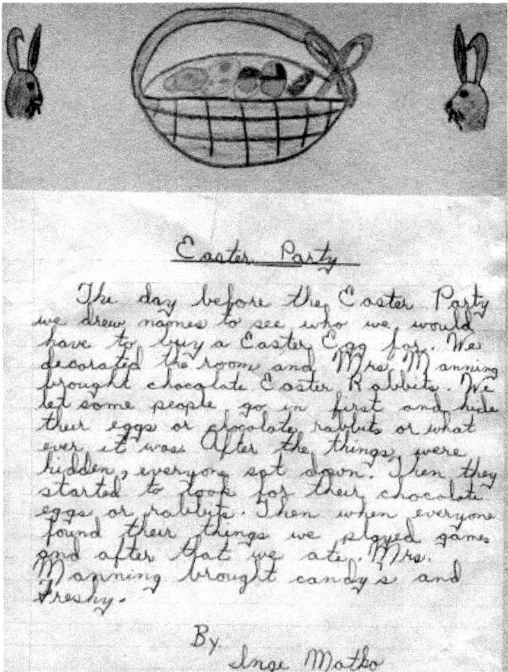

Page from scrap book Easter Party

Exams and the Easter Party

Having learned, from my too-long and arduous history and science exam questions in December, I spend extra time creating easier multiple-choice questions and a short essay question for each exam. Multiple-choice questions take twice as long to create but are much faster to mark. Because Easter holidays begin on Good Friday, March 27th, the Easter Party will need to be on March 26th. I need four days for exams, so they will occur on Friday and from the following Monday to

Wednesday. With the party on Thursday, I will defer marks until after the holiday.

For several weeks leading up to exams, I put examples on the board. As we work through them together, I explain, to the best of my ability, the most accurate way to decide which answer is correct.

When I explain to my students that they won't get exam marks back until after Easter holidays, no one seems particularly concerned. I'm hoping that, overall, the marks will be improved, not only in dreaded history and science but also spelling, math, and oral reading. It still amazes me that the grade ones are now reading and understanding words and sentences. Musical understanding, however, has improved only slightly, in spite of my extra work. Since I am the only one who seems perturbed about this, I keep it to myself.

With the promised Easter Party the day after exams, I know I must be organized ahead of time. On the weekend prior, I buy small chocolate Easter bunnies at Kresge's as well as several packets of Freshie, the latter stored in the back cupboard, the bunnies in my locked desk drawer. My helpers have informed me that there is always an Easter Hunt, and that we should draw names, the idea being that each student will have the name of another and will bring, for them, an edible Easter egg to school the day of the party. "And then," Susie says, eyes shining, "we all hide our eggs and hunt for them." The logistics of this I find challenging, and I ask how everyone will hide an egg without anyone else seeing. "You bring the kids in, one grade at a time," Marilyn says, seeming to sense my confusion, "so they can hide their eggs and go back outside. It usually works out okay." She and Susie set to work, printing everyone's name on small pieces of paper so the draw can take place.

That afternoon, before each person leaves, he or she draws a name from a cardboard box already decorated with paper Easter Eggs. I don't ask who prepared this, or when, now more accustomed to these small independent acts that have been part of a routine well in place before I arrived.

The following day, I shorten noon-hour to accommodate the egg hiding and, after all eggs are out of sight, call everyone in again.

The atmosphere is charged with no one sitting still; everyone is anticipating that the hunt will begin. I caution older students to watch out for little ones and help them if they don't find anything. On the count of three, the hunt begins. There are more than a few moments of pandemonium with fervour overriding sense, everyone dashing back and forth, crawling under desks and opening cupboard doors. Pencils and books are scattered, even a few coats and boots. It seems to me, however, that most students already know where their hidden egg is, as if, either they've been told, or it's in the same place it was last year. Given the rather limited places to hide things in our room, I surmise, but do not ask, that it is the latter. A few of the little ones end up in tears not being able to find their eggs anywhere until helped by someone else who knows where they are.

Once things calm down and some of the chocolate sampled, we play "I spy" with the younger children while games magically appear at a number of desks. I put art paper and crayons on the back table and encourage those not playing a game to draw pictures.

Several older students begin a game of monopoly while two more tackle chess. These games have obviously been brought in by those interested in playing them. I sense a tradition here, games that have been played many times, a comfortable routine on weekends perhaps, or over holidays. As an only child, I was never exposed to playing games, and I'm amazed by the co-operation and camaraderie that is generated. The room becomes almost quiet again and I walk about watching various strategies and moves unfold while handing out the chocolate bunnies. Two helpers have slipped to the back and are mixing Freshie. They go from group to group, giving drinks in paper cups to those who ask.

The room has slowly become dishevelled: empty paper cups and candy wrappers strewn about, desks moved to accommodate games, the floor sticky from spilled Freshie and squished chocolate. Fifteen minutes before dismissal, I ask that, grade by grade, the children put garbage in the waste paper basket and straighten desks. A few of the intense game players complain, but, overall, everyone co-operates. I wish everyone Happy Easter holidays and watch them hurry out, already chattering about what they will be doing during the week. Moments later, Mrs. Carr magically walks in and assures me she will clean the floor and set things right.

Oklahoma

CAST

Aunt Eller	VERNA TEMPLER
Curly	GEORGE CAMERON
Laurey	GWEN DUCHESNE
Ike Skidmore	DAVID ANDERSON
Fred	RAY SAUNDERS
Slim	DAVID COLLINS
Will Parker	RON CAMERON
Jud Fry	ART JONES
Ado Annie Carnes	LINDA MANNING
Ali Hakim	WESTLY WALTON
Gertie Cummings	KATHY KING
Ellen	LYNN CAMERON
Kate	DOROTHY BACON
Sylvie	PHYLLIS JONES
Armina	IRENE HARRIS
Terry	PEGGY ANDERSON
Aggie	ROBIN CLARK
Lizzie	MARY LOU HARRIS
Celia	NANCY WHITE
Vivian	JILL EDWARDS
Julie	PAT SHARPE
Andrew Carnes	BRUCE ANDERSON
Cord Elam	BILL REID
Jess	RALPH KNOX
Mike	RONALD KERR
IN THE BALLET: Laurey	PATRICIA HARRIS
Curly	ROY INGRAM
Jud	ART JONES

Program & Cast from this performance

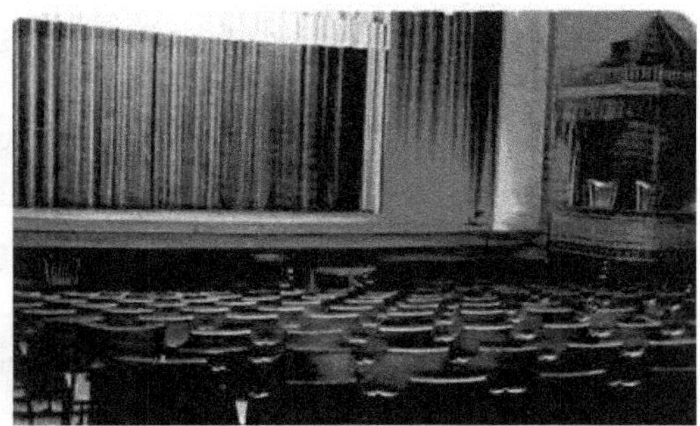

Victoria Opera House in the 1960's

Oklahoma Performance

It is an unforeseen blessing that the week of Easter holidays coincides with the week of the Oklahoma production in the Opera House of Victoria Hall. The dress rehearsal and four performances take up most of the week, and, each day, after settling Bruce at my feet with his Fisher Price garage and a number of Dinky toy cars and trucks, I manage to spend most mornings marking exams. Afternoons, after tucking him in for a nap, I brush up on lines or go outside to the old deciduous trees west of the house and sing the songs. Although it has been exhausting to juggle rehearsals, teaching and motherhood, "the smell of the greasepaint" has spurred me on. Our weekly rehearsals have created high expectations. Our not-so-great dress rehearsal, full of missed entrances and lines, is traditionally the omen of a good opening night. We get through it and hope for the best. I'm so keyed up opening day that I give up on trying to mark exams. Family and extended family are attending on Saturday night along with Jim. I have not said anything to my students, and no one has asked. There has been only one small ad in *The Cobourg Sentinel Star*, and, only a few, if any, of my students will likely attend. In some circles The Cobourg Opera and Drama Guild has an erudite, snobbish reputation even though Cobourg has long supported the Arts. This has been something I have been doing for myself, and if none of my students or parents attend the production, I will likely be relieved. I still worry a little whether my teacher's reputation will be sullied by playing this cheerfully promiscuous female, Ado Annie.

Opening night is exciting, nerve-wracking, and fantastic. The Opera House is packed right up to the first balcony. All my family are there except for dear Tante who has stayed home to look after Bruce. Jim takes innumerable pictures of the performance, and, after the last rousing chorus of "Oklahoma," we are cheered with a standing ovation and two curtain calls.

The following three performances are as successful as the first. I'd forgotten how intoxicating the "the smell of the grease paint and the roar of the crowd" is. After the last performance I feel a sense of loss at not having tried my hand at a stage career. I know that amateur theatre and professional theatre are completely different, and that "making it" in professional theatre is an incredibly long shot. One of those "what if" dreams never to be pursued.

At school, the following Monday, I get compliments from a number of the children who attended one of the performances with their parents. Several ask me how I managed to learn all the lines and several say I looked beautiful. Rather than being a detriment to my character as I feared, my role in Oklahoma has proven to be the opposite, an indication of my versatility and talent.

The following Thursday there is an article in the local paper, "Oklahoma in Victoria Opera House has Twenty-Seven in Cast." The article begins with general comments about the story followed by paragraphs outlining the role of each major character. Much praise is given to the two main leads with a relatively polite interpretation of my role, which suits me just fine.

My brief "star" performance quickly fades into the urgency of daily teaching and parental duties. Several weeks later, when Jim brings the developed photos home, my acting ability and creativity are again praised, but now the entire event and my role in it seem almost dream-like, something I did in another life. Reality is teaching, motherhood, and family. I deliberately chose these and am sure it is a choice for the best. I have no idea at this point in my life that, in fifteen years, my creativity will bring me to yet another career change, one that continues to this day.

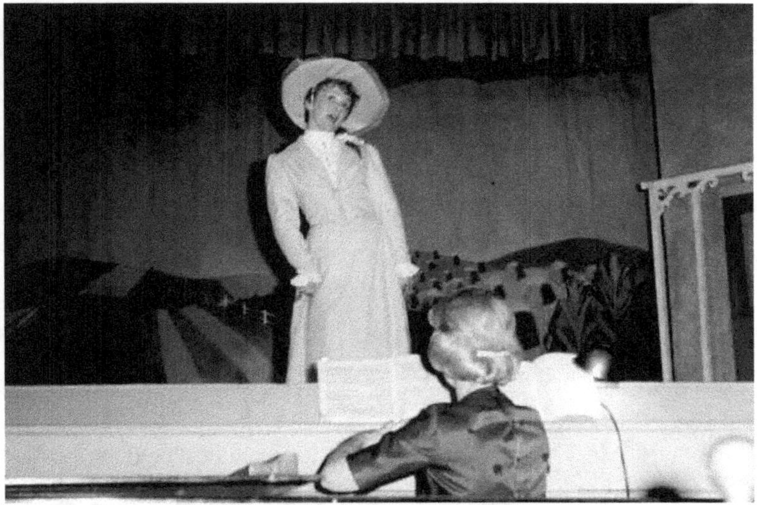

Ado Annie sings "I Cain't Say No"

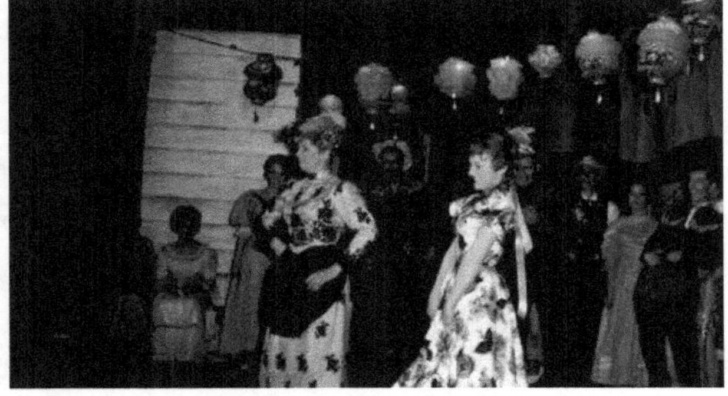

Aunt Eller (Verna Templer), Ado Annie and cast.

The Music Festival

On Monday before dismissal, after handing out report cards, I announce that we will, on Thursday when Mr. Thrip arrives, begin to prepare for the annual April Music Festival, this year to be held in the town of Warkworth. The announcement concerning this festival was on my desk when I arrived Monday morning, along with our category: "unison chorus in an ungraded school," the number given to us called "The Fairy Ring."

Even in the more conservative 1960's, I believe that only in an ungraded school would grade six and seven boys be charitable enough to sing a song bearing this title. During practice, each week, they stand with the rest of the grades one to seven, tripping lightly over staccato sixteenth note runs and, after several gentle lectures, manage not to look too excruciated, singing "We'll be fairies in the spring, dancing in a fairy ring."

As well, Mr. Thrip chooses four girls to sing a double duet: Marilyn, Susie, Irene, and her younger sister, Inge. Although their piece, "The Joy of Spring," seems old-fashioned, they work hard at it, practising at home as well as during our twice-a-week school practices for both duet and chorus. We also practice both pieces daily before dismissal.

Two weeks before our performance, Mr. Thrip announces that the Bluebirds who, up to this point, have been practising with the rest, are to be whisperers and should sing with almost no sound. He goes over the piece several times, and, with the Bluebirds almost silent, it does sound more melodic. At the end of the lesson, Mr. Thrip says he will provide piano accompaniment for both pieces and that we will meet in Warkworth. He adds that a school bus will pick us up at twelve noon sharp and that the children may bring a snack although it will have to be left in the bus.

The day of the Festival, when we arrive in Warkworth, most of my students are in their best clothes, all jittery and excited. As we file into the formidable church hall, we are ushered to our seats and cautioned to be quiet. I immediately recognize the dramatically-dressed woman at the podium on stage. It's Ruth Harcourt, recently back from an opera career in New York, now retired to look after her aging parents. I took singing lessons from Ruth when I was still in elementary school and hope to have a chance to speak to her later that afternoon. I know that she has been responsible for the revival of this Music Festival and listen as she enthusiastically welcomes everyone back for the afternoon session. She says school groups and individual songsters will be called up in turn and, scanning her list, announces the first category, solos and duets.

We sit for almost two hours listening to young voices, some too loud, some barely audible, and a few with a clear, musical sound. Our double duet is one of five in the category, and my four students sing the lyrics of "The Joy of Spring" with spirit, if not finesse. When Mr. Thrip strikes the final chord, I notice he looks quite pleased. There is little time to reflect as three more groups follow.

There are nine ungraded schools singing "The Fairy Ring" and some of them have not yet memorized the words so that, in sections, there is a mumble of sounds without clarity. We are second last, and, by the time I've listened to this chorus seven times, my tolerance level is at a low ebb. When the Front Road School West is finally called, the children, straightening their Sunday clothes, line up as we have practised, nervousness emanating from every face. Mr. Thrip plays the introduction, and my singers begin "The Fairy Ring." He is a skilled accompanist, nodding and waving an arm occasionally to accentuate rhythm, while my students sing with enthusiasm and gusto. In less than two minutes, it's over.

When the Adjudicator announces that we have won first in both categories, I'm astonished, and immediately, proud. Each child marches to the stage to receive a music certificate, with a larger one for me to frame and hang up in the school. On the way home, they insist on singing the song again, and this time it sounds almost perfect. Their excitement at winning continues and spills over as they leave the bus and head home. A number have parents waiting in cars, and several honk their horns upon hearing the news.

It's not until I'm home and sitting on the couch, trying to read to Bruce that I realize how tired I am. After a few pages of *One Fish Two Fish*, I feel myself drifting and beginning to doze. More than once, he pokes and jiggles my arm, rousing me to open my eyes and continue. At supper, I recount the day and our acquired accolades with Rosamonde and Tante who both congratulate me. "Part of our success," I say, "was Mr. Thrip, but most of it, my students."

"Most of it," Tante says quietly, "was you."

"And we're very proud of you," Rosamonde adds.

I nod, wishing I felt as confident about my teaching as they do.

There is always more to do than is possible, and I'm keenly aware that certain students have fallen behind because they need extra help that I have no time to provide. The days and weeks melt one into the other, and now—here it is—mid-April, and, before I know it, the year will be over.

Coming home after every school day, I feel the wrench of shifting from teacher to mother, from dealing with order and understanding to a certain degree of chaos and spontaneity. On this music concert evening, Bruce is particularly lively during his bath, splashing and making waves, coating my blouse, face, and hair with droplets of soapy water. It's a good thing I'm so tired it doesn't bother me. After another story, however, he's thankfully out like a light. I return downstairs to watch one of my favourite TV shows, *Maxwell Smart*, but after about five minutes, just when it's into the exciting part, I'm asleep again, waking only when

Maxwell sums up his latest detective achievement. Whatever marking I should be doing can wait. Sleep, at this point, is the only answer.

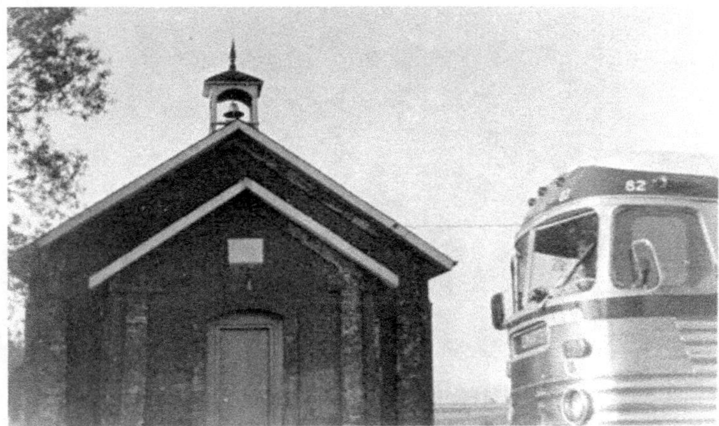

Bus to Music Festival

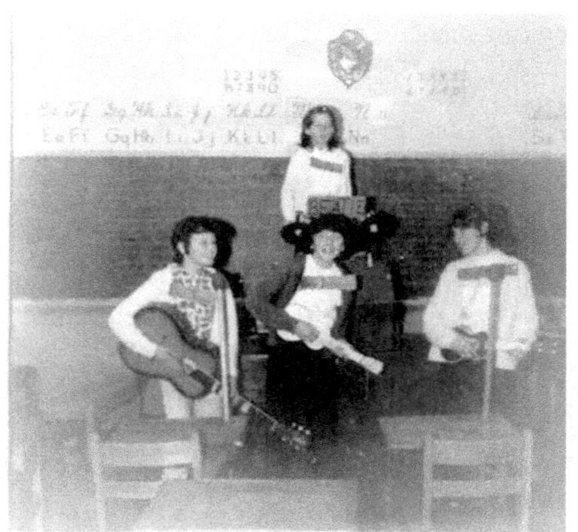

The "Beatles"

The Junior Red Cross and our Beatle's Concert

Back in September, I remember coming into school, one morning, to find a large manila envelope on my desk. Mrs. Carr must have brought it in from the mailbox.

The envelope contained several packets and a welcoming letter, inviting our class to join The Junior Red Cross Society. The letter included a short history of this society, saying it began in 1919 as a way to expose school children to the work and ideals of the Red Cross Society and that its membership now included just under a million Canadian students aged five to nineteen years old.

The letter suggested I devote one or more Friday afternoons a month to its activities. This would include student officers elected according to parliamentary procedure who would create and run a program following the Red Cross guidelines to undertake community service, school beautification programs, and correspond with Juniors in other countries. Monies raised could be sent to the Red Cross for the Crippled Children's Fund. Included in the package was a national Junior Red Cross magazine, membership pins, cards for each student, and a cardboard Donation Box.

It all looked amazing and wonderful, but I knew we could not formally support this organization. There was no extra time during the week for this activity no matter how just and noble it seemed.

That afternoon, before dismissal, I produced the envelope and talked to the children about the organization. I gave each child a pin and a membership card, put the magazine on my desk for anyone to look at, and explained that the donation box on my desk was for the Crippled Children's Fund. I read from the letter that "this was one of the Junior Red Cross goals, to help those less fortunate," and, that if anyone had extra pennies during the year, I planned to leave the box on my desk for small donations.

The next morning, well before class, a parent was at the door, looking decidedly disgruntled. When I invited him in, he shook his head and remained on the front step.

"You gave these out to my youngins," he began, shoving two Red Cross pins and membership cards into my hand. "We don't want'm."

"There's no cost," I said, feeling at a loss to understand where this conversation was heading.

"I don't give no money to furiners," he continued, "crippled or not."

"The card and the membership button are free," I added, "it's the Red Cross Society."

"Nope," he cut me off. "I'd give ya money for the kids here but that's it." He turned and stomped back toward his car.

I wasn't even sure which of my children were his. After comforting a grade-one student who fell coming up the steps, finishing seat work on the board, and getting the morning started, I forgot all about the man.

Over the months, the box is pushed aside and moved and ends up beside the chalk box at one side of the front blackboard. Whenever I notice it, I feel a little guilty, thinking I should be helping the children organize something, but what? And when? The days and weeks fly by with lessons and deadlines and exams.

A week after the excitement of the Music Festival has subsided and our school routine is again running on an even keel, Marilyn, Inge, Irene and Susie surround my desk on a Monday noon hour.

"You know how we listen to the Beatles all the time?" Susie begins.

"And we sing along to their songs?" Irene adds.

"We were wondering," Inge who is Irene's younger sister says, giving me her delightful smile, "if…" She stops, seeming unsure whether she should continue.

"If we could," Marilyn cuts in, looking overly serious, "put on a Beatles Concert."

"We thought we could do it to raise money for the Junior Red Cross," Irene adds.

"The Junior Red Cross," I say. "We certainly haven't done anything for them all year."

"That's why we thought it would be a good idea," Marilyn goes on, "we could invite parents and younger kids. Have it in the afternoon and take up a donation for the Crippled Children's Fund."

I'm impressed they even remember this and look around to see where the Donation Box is.

Irene retrieves it and, giving it a jiggle, puts it back on my desk. "A few of us," she says, "have been putting money in the box."

"We read about children with polio," Susie adds, "in that magazine, and we wanted to do something."

"So you thought of a Beatles concert?" I add. Anything to have more Beatles' songs, I think, smiling.

"Maybe a week from next Friday, in the afternoon?"

"A Beatles concert in two weeks," I say, looking at the four of them. It would be hard to say no, given their success at the Music Festival.

They call their event, *Beatlemania,* and make up invitations which they give out a week before the show. The invitations say there will be a goodwill donation after the show and that the money will go to The Junior Red Cross. I remember the disgruntled parent who complained in September and wonder if this is a good idea. However, given the girls are so wound up and excited, I decide to keep this reservation to myself.

Irene says they've been practising since before the Music Festival. They have an old guitar and have borrowed younger classmate Sheila's toy ukulele, but still need another stringed instrument. I, luckily, have a ukulele which I promise to bring to school for them. Irene's younger sister is to be the drummer using, she explains, large wooden spoons, one of our wooden chair seats, with a tambourine and cymbals tied to its legs.

All week, there's a buzz about the upcoming performance. On Wednesday, Marilyn asks me if her Mom can attend to take pictures. On Thursday, over noon hour, the girls do a technical rehearsal which involves moving furniture and setting up the "chair-to-be-drum set" on my cleared desk. They've obviously been working hard at all this, and I'm impressed by their ingenuity and enthusiasm.

The day of the show, the four girls spend all noon hour making name tags: Marilyn is George, Irene is John, Susie is Paul, and Inge is Ringo. They push my desk close to the blackboard with the designated drum chair backwards on top. Inge has tied the tambourine and cymbal to the front chair legs, and a large "Beatlemania" sign is fastened to its back. Inge stands behind on another chair, and will pound the chair seat, the cymbal, and tambourine with her wooden spoons. The three instrumentalists manoeuvre broom handles, each topped with a rubber bulb, through the inkwell holes of three desktops, respectively, and the technical setup is complete.

The excitement, when school resumes that afternoon, makes it difficult to accomplish much. I defer going over history questions with grades five to seven and decide not to hear reading from the grade fours. Instead, we have an art lesson where I prop up the ukuleles and guitar on separate window ledges and invite the children to draw one of them or their favourite instrument. Some students, of course, finish this in less than a half an hour while others are still hard at it after an hour. I invite several to show the class their drawing and talk about their chosen instrument. John and Keith give us some interesting facts about trumpets and trombones while Cathy Burnham tells us about their family piano and how it is tuned.

During afternoon recess, the four musicians huddle together, going over song titles written on a piece of paper. They tell me they are doing six numbers, two sets of three with a short break between. They fill glasses of tap water and put them on the east window ledge explaining that they will need a drink at the break. Susie checks the mop handle mics, and Inge makes sure everything is fastened securely on the drum setup. Marilyn produces a hand mirror, and the three of them spend several minutes each carefully combing their hair forward almost covering their eyes. Inge, whose hair is too long, is the exception, and Irene explains it won't matter as she's at the back anyway. Finally, huddling together, giggling and whispering, they tell me they are ready. As I ring the bell to bring everyone in, Marilyn's mom, who lives across the street, slips in, getting her camera ready as everyone is taking off their coats.

Beatlemania is an overwhelming success. Other than for the improvised drum set, the songs are sung a capella with a minimal non-melodic strumming of instruments. The four girls do amazingly well; not one lyric is missed, and their infrequent strumming is barely noticed. Beginning with "I Want to Hold Your Hand," they transition to "PS. I Love You" and end the set with "Love Me Do." My usually sensible students are wound to a fever pitch, some singing along, some cheering, and one or two screaming. At the break, I ask everyone to stand, and we go through a march-on-the-spot and clap routine designed to burn off some of the built-up energy and excitement. Even Mrs. Moore joins in.

The second set begins with "Twist and Shout" which prompts spontaneous dancing; "Can't Buy Me Love" thankfully quiets things down and "It's Been a Hard Day's Night" has almost all of them singing along. After thunderous applause, someone shouts "encore," and everyone pounds their desks, repeating the request in rhythm. The girls whisper, momentarily, then begin where they started with "I Want to Hold Your Hand." Wild clapping and a standing ovation that lasts several minutes ends the concert.

When everyone calms down, Marilyn announces she will have the Junior Red Cross donation box at the door and hopes there will be some contributions. After everyone leaves and the girls are putting the desks and chairs back in place, I open the box. Three one dollar bills and a handful of change totals $5.24. I'm impressed and tell them I will go to the post office for a money order to send to the Red Cross.

Before they leave, Susie asks me if she can print something on the blackboard. I say yes, assuming it will be about the Beatles or the concert. In large printed letters she writes: THE FRONT ROAD SCHOOL RAISED $5.24 FOR THE JUNIOR RED CROSS!

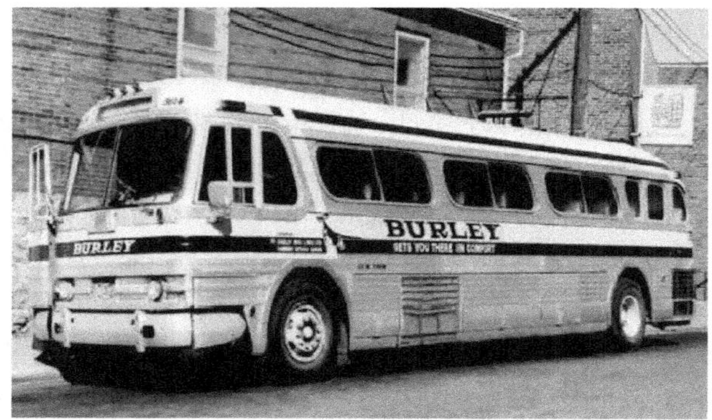

Burley Bus (*Photo Credit: Port Hope District Historical Society*)

Organizing A School Trip

For some time now, I have been thinking about taking my students on a school trip. It will have to be at the beginning of June as final exams must be set and results in at least a week before school ends on June 26th. I have nothing to go on and nowhere to ask but I do remember when I was in Baltimore Public School from 1950 to 1953 that Miss Hogg took us, her senior class, on a boat trip to the Thousand Islands in the St. Lawrence River and to Old Fort Henry in Kingston.

Before dismissal, that day, I ask Marilyn to ask her dad how I would go about arranging a class excursion that included a bus trip. Marilyn, of course, wants to know if I am planning a trip for the class and I tell her I am considering it but will have to find out about cost before talking to everyone. The next morning she comes to me with a slip of paper on which is written: Burley Bus Lines, Ontario St. She grins and puts her fingers to her lips signifying she's keeping my secret.

After school, that day, I drop in at the Burley Bus Lines Office where the secretary, Bernadette Gatien, not only gives me details regarding bus cost but also says she will contact the Thousand Island Boat Tours and Old Fort Henry for school trip prices.

A few days later, when I receive this information and add up the cost, even though I will get a school group rate, I worry the cost per student will be too high. I talk this over with Mr. Moore, my Board contact, and he says it's reasonable to ask for five dollars per student. I know many of the parents make substantially less than I do and that for some families this will be a huge sacrifice. The average wage in Canada at this time is about $1500 per year, or roughly $30 a week. Five dollars could easily represent a good part of a week's groceries.

I decide to discuss the cost with the class, and before dismissal on Friday tell them what I would like to do, realizing that most of the children will have no idea what their family income is. Everyone is enthusiastic and hands shoot up with a myriad of suggestions. The best advice comes from children who previously attended town schools. Both Wolfgang and Allan say that their schools had raffles to raise money for a trip. When I ask for more details, they tell me that, in one case, a small item of furniture was raffled and in another, a painting. I know the school board won't be able to purchase anything for a raffle, and when I ask how we would acquire an item to raffle, several students say not to worry, they will ask their parents.

The following Monday, Allan reports that his Dad knows one of the local merchants and he's sure something can be arranged. On Wednesday, Allan arrives with a large table lamp, its china base the shape of a vase, its shade a pale yellow. After some class discussion, we decide twenty-five cents is a reasonable ticket price, and, after recess that afternoon, instead of regular classes, I give the grade one and two's a colouring activity and put the grade three to seven's to work making raffle tickets. On the board, I print:

RAFFLE TICKET 25 cents
FOR OUR SCHOOL TRIP
THOUSAND ISLANDS BOAT TOUR & OLD FORT HENRY

I hand out seven strips of pre-cut paper to each child and instruct them to copy this information saying that I will number the tickets and hand them out tomorrow. Most of the tickets turn out reasonably, a few with extra flourishes, and after making a few more tickets of my own, I end up with 130.

I write up a letter to send home explaining the trip:

Dear parent,

I am hoping to arrange a school trip to the Thousand Islands and Old Fort Henry for the first week of June. In order to reduce the cost per student, we are planning to have a raffle, the prize, a new table lamp, has been donated.

If you could help in any way, I would greatly appreciate it.
Sincerely,
Mrs. Manning, teacher and principal
The Front Road School West

I carefully print the letter onto a piece of paper and copy it to a coated mimeograph stencil paper before reproducing it. I have created seat work this way and know I must press hard on the paper in order to break the paper seal so that when placed on the mimeograph rotating drum, the ink will permeate where pressed and create the master stencil. There are a limited number of blank stencil sheets, and I must go slowly and carefully. Once finished, I attach this stencil to the ink-saturated surface of the machine's hollow, rotating cylinder. I turn the handle on one side of the cylinder, and, as it rotates, ink flows through the cuts in the stencil to the sheets of paper fed under the cylinder. The smell of ink is acrid and distinctive as anyone who has used one of these machines knows. I make fifteen copies for the families in the school, laying them out on back desks to dry.

On Friday before dismissal, I tell everyone we must sell at least 100 tickets and ask that one member of each family take a copy of the letter and as many tickets as they think they can sell. Thankfully, all tickets are picked up, and I'm quite sure, several children took only one while others a handful.

By Wednesday of the following week, all ticket stubs are back in, and, on Friday, we draw the winning ticket. I am pleased to tell everyone we have raised thirty dollars which will pay for the bus and maybe more. I ask Joe Harper, as the eldest student present, to draw the winning ticket. He reaches into the box scrunches the stubs long enough to get sighs and several "Hurry ups" from the class. The winning ticket is John Wilson's. He raises a triumphant fist in the air and shouts, "yes."

On Friday, Bernadette from Burley Bus lines calls the Manning residence to say the trip is arranged and that I am to pick up tickets for both the boat trip and Old Fort Henry at each site. When I talk to her on Monday after school, she says the bus cost will be $28.50 and the cost of the two outings $133.95. If I can pay for everything, in advance, it will make things easier once I get to the destinations. Bernadette will give me receipts which I can exchange for the tickets. I haven't yet finalized how much to charge each student, and that evening I phone Mr. Moore to ask his advice. I have already figured out that if I ask for five dollars from each person going on the trip plus the raffle money, I will have almost enough. He says the Board could donate ten dollars so that I'm sure to have enough. I will have to pay for the trip and go on trust, collecting the money from my students later. Some of them, I know, will not be able to pay until right before we go.

On Monday, I tell everyone that the price for the trip including the bus, a ticket to Old Fort Henry, and the Boat Tour will be five dollars per student. Most nod in agreement but I can see that a few look worried. I tell them I must pick the tickets up soon and will pay for the trip out of my own money less the thirty dollar raffle money and a ten-dollar donation from the Board. I say I would like the money by the end of May at the latest. I can only hope that most will be able to pay their way as I don't want anyone to be excluded. The trip is a month away and we must now return to the business of day-to-day lessons.

The following week, however, an unexpected visitor not only livens up our school routine but also demands 24/7 attention.

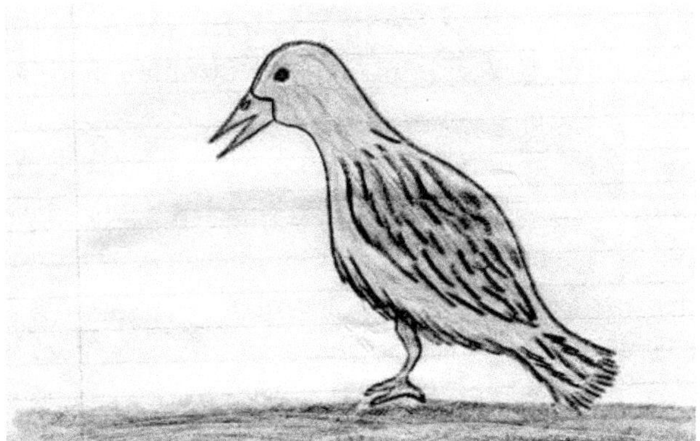

Drawing of Rebel. (Artist: Wolfgang Hofer)

The Story of Rebel

With the rainy weather of April past, May brings warmer weather and enough wind to dry up both the baseball field and our school yard. Farmers in neighbouring fields are ploughing where it's not too wet, and my students are outside at both recess and noon hour.

Even on the coldest winter days, some children always arrive early at school and I assume it's because their parents have already left for work. During the winter and into wet spring, these children have come inside to warm up or dry out, venturing back out when other classmates arrive. This is one of the reasons I have made sure I am at the school by 7:30 each morning. Although Wayne and, his sister, Debbie are often the first to arrive, now, that the warmer weather has arrived, they pop in only briefly to deposit their lunches, returning immediately outside.

Just east of the school, a creek runs from a culvert under the highway past our building and on toward Lake Ontario. The creek is off limits being beyond school property, but some students, usually older boys, go there in spring to investigate. Someone always tells on them and, as I discourage tattling, I rarely punish any who do. Besides, the west side, with its baseball diamond and expansive field, is usually preferred.

There are no trees near the school except one large deciduous hardwood, its towering trunk and ragged branches close to the highway west of us. Along the creek, however, it's a different matter, with one old gnarled tree that leans south and a few smaller Elms following the creek bed further along. During fall months, we occasionally heard bird trills through the open windows but I've never noticed birds or nests anywhere in the immediate vicinity.

On a Friday morning in May, I notice the Simpson children have arrived, even earlier than usual. Through the open windows, their chatter moves from the west side of the school to the east, but, as I'm busy getting history questions on the board, I barely notice. A short time later, I hear a bicycle wheel up and I know it's likely Wolfgang.

The front door opens and Debbie rushes in. "Mrs. Manning, Mrs. Manning, Wayne has found a baby bird, and Wolfgang wants to bring it inside."

I follow her to the cement stoop and find Wolfgang cradling a fledgling baby bird, its wide yellow beak opening and closing. "It's a starling," Wolfgang says, "and I know it's hungry."

John and Keith Wilson wheel in on their bikes with Keith, coming over to have a look. "A dumb starling," he says with some derision, "we should kill it. My dad says there's too many starlings around here."

Wolfgang folds his fingers protectively over the starling and says, with conviction beyond his years, "It can't help being born a starling. I say we should save it."

Keith shrugs, and he and his brother slip inside to retrieve the bat and ball. "Who cares about a dumb bird," Keith adds, striding back outside. "Come on, let's play ball."

"It must have fallen out of its nest," Wolfgang continues. "Wayne says he saw it huddled against the east wall."

By now, several other students have arrived, and everyone is inspecting the starling, most with positive comments. "If we could find a cardboard box," Wolfgang says, moving closer to the door, "we could bring him inside."

"Bring him in," I say, smiling that the bird has been categorized as a male already. "I'm sure there's a box in the storage room."

By the time we are inside the classroom, Wayne has rushed ahead and produces a suitable cardboard box from the storeroom.

"Our starling needs a name," I say. "Wayne, you found the bird, what should we call him?"

"I don't know." Wayne looks at Wolfgang. "What do you think we should call him?"

Wolfgang looks at the bird, now settled in his hands, eyes closed. "He's a rebel surviving a fall from his nest. We should call him Rebel." As soon as he places Rebel in the box, he livens up, chirping and flapping his boney wings.

Marilyn arrives and, after admiring Rebel, says she'll go back to her house across the road, for an eye dropper. "To give him water," she says, "until he learns how to drink from a bowl."

Wolfgang disappears outside and returns shortly with a wriggling earthworm. "Anyone who is squeamish better leave," he says, to those still huddled around the box. "I'll have to cut this worm into pieces."

Squeals and groans follow, and most observers dash outside. "It's the same as when we go fishing," he says, looking at me, "it has to be done."

I go to the board and continue with seat work. Watching a worm being cut up is not something I wish to experience.

Marilyn returns with the eye dropper and is pleased that Rebel dutifully opens his beak and swallows several servings of water. Wolfgang brings the worm bits on a paper towel and is rewarded for his efforts, for Rebel opens his mouth over and over until the entire worm is gone. I suggest putting the paper towel in the bottom of the box, partly to give the bird's claws traction and partly to make the box easier to clean.

"It's nearly nine," I say. "Better put the box on top of the piano." I have no idea how long we can keep our new addition but decide I will deal with this later.

After opening ceremonies, I put the box on the piano bench, and, grade by grade, those who have not been introduced to Rebel, come and say hello. This works reasonably well, although the excitement of having a resident bird in the room causes extra chatter off and on until recess.

For our Friday afternoon art class, I ask everyone to draw a picture of Rebel either before or after he came to us. The results are interesting and, in the case of a few, highly imaginative. A number of drawings show Rebel huddled against the side of the school while a few depict him falling or jumping from his nest. Wolfgang, our resident artist, draws the detailed likeness included in this chapter.

At the end of the day, we spend fifteen minutes talking about who will look after Rebel during the day and overnight. As both Marilyn and Wolfgang offer, I decide we will postpone this decision until next week. Wolfgang says he will prepare worms daily, and it is suggested that hard boiled eggs may also work. Someone will have to take him home each day after school and on the weekend. I have no idea, at this point, how long it will take before the bird will be able to return to its natural habitat. I offer to look after him this weekend.

Once home, I put Rebel and his box on the Manning's closed-in back porch. Bruce is, of course, fascinated and wants to play with this baby bird. When I explain he can only look, he soon loses interest. As I'm not prepared to hunt and chop worms, we try a hard-boiled egg and find that Rebel gobbles it up with no problem. On Saturday morning, I realize I will have to change the paper towel liner several times a day, and make a mental note to take an extra roll to school on Monday. Rebel is a nonstop eater and chirps loudly for food on the hour. On Sunday morning, I add bread to his egg and water diet and, in the afternoon, when I take toys outside to play with Bruce, I put the box nearby in a sunny spot. Rebel seems to enjoy this and gives himself a thorough cleaning.

In spite of the fact that having a bird in the class is a major distraction, his ongoing care the following week runs smoothly and doesn't deter most students from getting their daily lessons and seat work completed. Occasionally, when someone is reading aloud, they will pause to stare in Rebel's chirping direction long enough to lose his or her place. Several times during spelling dictation, one or two will ask for a word to be repeated. As soon as we begin talking, Rebel likes to join in. To him, it seems, we are large and noisy nest mates.

Wolfgang takes over as chief organizer. He has brought a wicker basket and transfers Rebel to it each noon hour, taking him out for sun and compromising his participation in baseball. He has selected several of the younger boys to dig for worms along the creek bank, making sure Rebel's voracious appetite is served. Following the weekend, Rebel is swallowing whole worms with no problem, on the hour, every hour. After school each day, Wolfgang fastens an old tee shirt over the top of the basket and takes Rebel home on his bike.

On Tuesday, it appears Rebel is already outgrowing his box. I am currently reading *Gulliver's Adventures in Brobdingnag* to the children and so Wolfgang, copying the travelling carrier that Gulliver was put into by the giants when at Court, fashions a better box with six small windows and a rope handle.

Wednesday, Mr. Thrip bursts in as he always does and, before I can say anything, is at the piano, singing and playing the latest song he wants the class to learn. Rebel has just been fed and remains quiet. Soon, however, the piano's vibrations and the singing prompt him to join in, first from inside his box and then, for the first time, hopping onto its edge, looking quizzically down at everyone. When this happens, Mr. Thrip stops in mid-chord, emitting a small startled noise. Wolfgang runs to him and begins a rapid-fire explanation of finding the bird and how we are looking after him.

Mr. Thrip seems mildly amused and carries on with the lesson but does point out to me, before he leaves, that birds are dirty things and shouldn't be allowed inside. I assure him it's a temporary measure and that the fledging will likely be gone the following Wednesday.

On Thursday, Rebel makes history by flying the distance of ten inches from his box to Wolfgang's outstretched hand. It's clear to all of us that Wolfgang is the bird's surrogate parent. Once Rebel realizes he can get out of the box, he spends the rest of the day exploring the top of the piano, picking at a bouquet of flowers and anything else available. Wolfgang puts the bird's water bowl on the piano top and, for the first time, Rebel drinks from it, eliciting a cheer from the class. Seeming pleased with his new found ability, he jumps into the water dish for a bath. Wolfgang hurriedly closes the piano lid to protect the keys and mops up splashed water and other deposits the bird has left behind.

On Friday afternoon, as I'm reading about Gulliver becoming disenchanted with the Brogdingnagians and life at Court, Rebel surprises and delights everyone by flying from his box to the far side of the room, landing unceremoniously on the table beside the sink. The children applaud, and Wolfgang rushes to return the bird to his piano top lookout. Rebel settles down and doesn't attempt another flight that day.

On Monday, Wolfgang recounts to the class Rebel's escapades over the weekend. "Saturday was okay," he begins. "I went fishing with my Dad, and my sister looked after Rebel for the day. Sunday is another story." He paused, looking intently at us, and I could see the beginning of a storyteller emerging. "We all went fishing," he continues, "the whole family, and Dad wouldn't let me take Rebel as he felt he would be in the way. I left him with a pile of worms and an egg and hoped he would be okay." He pauses again and most of the younger ones are now sitting forward on their seats. "When we arrived home, we couldn't find Rebel anywhere." He gives an arm flourish. "Dad was not pleased and Mom didn't like the idea of the bird flying around her clean house. Finally, we found him caught up behind the curtain of a living room window. He wasn't hurt, but I could tell my parents were losing their patience. My mom spent over an hour cleaning up after him. I'm not sure what will happen next weekend." Before he sits down, everyone claps, and he gives a courtly bow.

Flying is now Rebel's primary goal. He flits back and forth, often landing on someone's head or on an open book. When taken outside at recess, he flies into a tree and chirps pitifully to be rescued—three times in fifteen minutes. I know we will have to do something soon, *what* being the quintessential dilemma.

Tuesday, before we leave, Wolfgang asks if he can speak to the class. His seriousness ripples through the room, and when he comes to the front, all I can hear is everyone's quiet breathing. "I've talked to Marilyn," he begins, a catch in his voice, "and we've decided to let Rebel go free in her back yard this evening." There is complete silence until one of the younger girls, sobs audibly. "He is a wild bird," Wolfgang continues, "he should not be caged."

The next morning, after opening exercises, the room seems too quiet, no box on the piano, no chirping anywhere in the room. Wolfgang and Marilyn come to the front and finish the story. "My Dad took me over to Marilyn's after supper," he says, "and when I opened the box, Rebel flew directly onto Marilyn's head." Several giggles ensue. Marilyn continues. "After a few minutes, he flew up into a nearby tree. It was beginning to get dark and so we couldn't see exactly where he was. I told Wolfgang he could go home and that I would look for him in the morning." She sniffles and squares her shoulders. "He was gone this morning, and my Mom says that's a good thing, that's where he belongs."

The two of them sit down and the morning's work takes over everyone's attention. Once in a while, though, I notice someone staring toward the piano. Our hands-on nature lesson has come to an end, a good end. The bird survived and everyone learned how demanding and relentless a mother bird's life must be, the endless search for food and the dangers and pitfalls inherent in pushing one's offspring toward independence. We are, hopefully, wiser from this experience and, perhaps, slightly more tolerant.

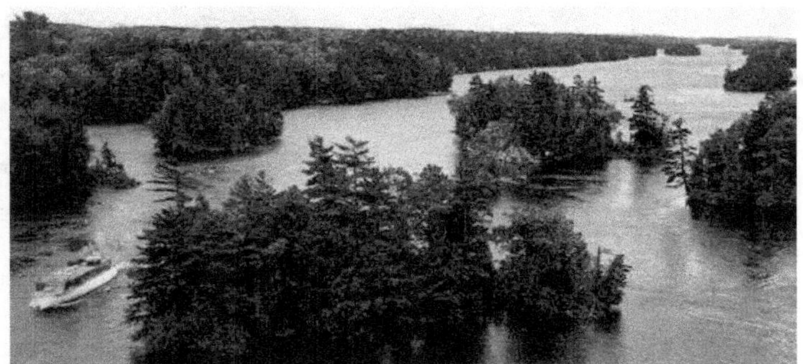

Thousand Islands

Trip to the Thousand Islands

The week of the trip, I am relieved that all families have been able to pay their way. I did find out that several children spent time each day, after school, scouring both sides of the road for empty bottles to trade, in order to secure enough money for the trip. They would likely take them to Nick and Ethel's garage with its candy counter and pop cooler. Apparently there is a hole in the fence opposite the garage parking lot, and students often sneak through in order to get candy at noon, another of the clandestine, outdoor activities I never knew about.

Four parents will accompany us on this trip and I have asked everyone to bring a packed lunch. From Monday to Thursday of the chosen week, excitement builds. I feel badly that the grade one and twos are excluded but am sure much of the trip would bore them. Most of them seem to be looking forward to a full day holiday from school.

The bus will pick us up at 7 a.m. sharp on June 5th and I have asked everyone to be there by 6:30 a.m. I've never been to the school this early, and, with the sun low on the eastern horizon, the school playground is covered in sparkly dew. Even though the excitement and pent up energy is palpable, I insist that the children, most in their best clothes, stay in front of the school. Some stand in small groups, some with a parent, one or two pacing back and forth. I open the school so that whoever needs to can use the toilets. Some of these children have never been on a bus, as the extent of their travelling has been by car no further than nearby Port Hope or Cobourg.

As soon as the bus slows down in front of the school, everyone lines up as if going into class. I'm grateful that two mothers and a couple of children have cameras. I climb into the bus first and am greeted by our friendly bus driver who announces that we'll be going on Highway Two all the way. "There's a couple of stretches of the new Highway 401 east of here, but it's not worth driving up and back to connect."

I position myself in the front seat so I can stand and talk to the students if needed. Everyone sits more quietly than I anticipate. The strangeness of it all is intimidating for many.

Once we're on our way, however, chattering begins with comments on houses we see, the size of farms and stands of trees. We pass through innumerable small towns and villages, and gleeful comments are made about us being on the road while everyone else is in school.

The rock formations on either side of the highway coming into Kingston are impressive, and Allan says that some rocks are millions of years old. This is received with several snorts of disbelief, and I think to myself that researching it would make such a good geography project. The problem is we have no reference books at the school, and asking students to go to the Cobourg or Port Hope Library is out of the question. It's one of the frustrating parts of my job. and, most of the time, I simply ignore it. The graded schools I visited when "practice teaching" (Appendix 5), all had libraries with a good selection of nonfiction and fiction titles. I stare out the window. Better to concentrate on this trip, on my students, and on what we can accomplish today.

As we enter the Kingston city limits, the bus driver informs me we're stopping at the Kingston bus depot. "A pit stop," he says, smiling. "I know how youngsters are. There're washrooms and a tuck shop."

Driving through Kingston is itself an education for my students: houses, apartment buildings, and, closer to the lake, a more industrial area with lumber yards, factories and the cramped back yards of narrow row housing. Laundry on lines, tethered dogs, the occasional small garden, rusting cars and bicycles are all eye-openers for many of my students, even the poorer ones whose houses are on large lots, usually back from the highway, with fields behind.

The Kingston bus depot is large and noisy with that ever present smell of exhaust fumes. The children stay close together, barely talking, as we make our way into the building. Everyone wants to use the washroom, and only those who make it in and out quickly have time to look at what is available to buy. The few who have spending money buy Kingston souvenirs or candy. From here to the Kingston docks is not too far. We've been on the bus for nearly three hours. As we approach the docks, I caution everyone to stay together and hold hands with an older sibling or friend if nervous. The bus driver tells me he is dropping us off at the bottom of Brock St and that he will be back for us in four and a half hours.

Our boat, the Miss Kingston, lies rocking gently close to the docks. Painted white with red trim, she looks regal and elegant against the blue river-water backdrop. The first level is closed in with open windows for viewing. The upper deck has a substantial railing and, close to the front, is the Captain's wheelhouse, closed-in with more windows. A set of stairs beside it allows guests to watch from a smaller area at the prow of the ship. I have never been close to a river boat of this size and am as impressed by it, as are my students.

A number of other school groups are lining up to go on this boat cruise, and the noise level is deafening. I leave the children clustered with our adults and make my way to the ticket booth. The ticket lady, in a nautical uniform, hands me a large envelope and I hurry back to distribute the tickets, cautioning each child to hang on tightly if they want to get on the boat. We are instructed to stand in lines, one beside the other, and that we will be instructed when to board. One of the school groups is quite rowdy, and our children stare at their antics in disbelief. I look at the teacher and feel a wave of sympathy, remembering my student teacher days.

Once the lines begin to move, expectation builds, a few of the younger ones jumping up and down in excitement. We quickly find a section of empty seats and watch as the others stream past. Several of the older boys want to go upstairs to the second level right away, but I say they can always go up there once we're moving and that they're better to stay where we are. The windows have no glass and I tell everyone to be careful, to look out the window but not to lean out too far. The boat rocks gently and warm breezes pull in the smell of lake, wet docks, and diesel fuel. Children from another group are already running up and down the aisle, and I'm proud of my well-behaved children.

A voice booms "All aboard," and a loud horn sounds. The boat shudders and begins to move slowly into the harbour. The Captain's voice comes over the loud speaker, welcoming us aboard the Miss Kingston. He says, "She was built in 1942 and operated as a Canadian Navy coastal patrol boat. In 1960 she was converted into the cruise boat we are on today."

With two to a seat, only one child is close to a window. The younger ones squish in side by side while older children decide to have one seated with one standing behind, often leaning over the other's shoulder. As we list to one side and then the other, someone calls out that it's like Gulliver when he was out to sea. I'm momentarily overwhelmed, realizing I have actually pulled this trip off, that my class is here on the Thousand Islands Boat Tour.

When I suggest we should have lunch, everyone agrees and there is relative quiet for the next fifteen minutes. Three of the senior girls ask if they can go to the snack bar in the rear, and I notice a few younger ones tagging along with them. Mothers take turns going up to the second deck with the younger ones, and I am more than pleased to sit and keep track of those remaining.

The first notable places we pass are Old Fort Henry on the left and Wolfe Island on the right. The fort's grey, stone walls are intimidating even from this distance. Our Captain points out ramparts and cannons and two of the Martello Towers. Once we're past the Fort, several older students come rushing down the stairs with questions. "How old is it?" "What's a Martello Tower?" "Why was the fort built here?" "Who fought battles and why?" I retrieve one of the pamphlets from the envelope that has a brief history and description of the fort.

"It was originally built during the war of 1812," I begin. "The British, who controlled the Colonies as they were called, were afraid the Americans would attack and capture the naval dock yards and cut off an important trading route."

"And did they?" someone asks.

"It says they did not," I continue, "but, apparently, the presence of the fort likely stopped them from trying."

"So, no battles?" one of the boys adds, sounding disappointed.

"I'm sure we'll find out more when we visit," I add, "and I know there will be someone you can ask."

Most students drift off, again, more interested in the numerous elegant houses with long wooden docks, most of them isolated between extensive stretches of woodland. Many of the children have never seen homes this large, and, I hear discussion as to whether the houses are that large because the families living in them have so many children, or whether they are extremely rich and have rooms for lots of servants and guests.

Once past Howe Island and the city of Gananoque, the towering International Bridge appears, spanning from one side of the river to the other. The Captain explains that it's actually a series of bridges which connect Canada to the United States and that during the peak tourist season there is always a one to two-hour wait to drive across. A number of students rush up to the open deck to view it better, and several who stay below say they wouldn't want to drive across it—too high up and too scary.

Next, we see the towers of Boldt Castle situated on Heart Island in American waters. The Captain tells us it was built at the turn of the century by George C. Boldt, the millionaire proprietor of the world-famous Waldorf Astoria Hotel. He says that Boldt set out to build a full-size Rhineland Castle as a display of love for his wife, Louise. Three hundred workers fashioned the six-storey, 120 room castle, and not a single detail or expense was spared. Unfortunately, in 1904, Boldt's wife died suddenly, and all construction was halted. Boldt never returned to the island, leaving behind the unfinished structure as a monument to his love. The Captain adds that it is currently owned by the Thousand Islands Bridge Authority that is restoring the castle to its intended glory. The senior girls find this incredibly romantic and chatter on about it until the boys head upstairs in disgust.

Not far past Rockport, the Captain comes back on to say we should look for two small islands, the Zavikons, with a thirty-two-foot footbridge between them. He goes on to say that, a popular but incorrect tale says the larger island is in Canada, while "Little Zavikon Island" is in the United States. This makes the footbridge between them the "shortest international bridge in the world."

Someone asks me why this would be called something it is not and isn't that lying? I have to say "Yes, it is, but like a number of things we read about in history, at some point, the truth is altered and becomes a tall tale." This would make such a good class discussion, especially for the seniors, but I know this is neither the time nor place to begin. Besides, as the boat glides on, another landmark comes into sight, and everyone is distracted or has forgotten the question altogether.

At the two-hour point, the boat makes a slow turning arc and begins heading back toward Kingston, weaving through yet another set of islands. The Captain tells us there are 1,864 islands ranging in size from some that are more than forty square miles to smaller islands occupied by a single residence, to uninhabited outcroppings of rocks. To count as one of the Thousand Islands, there must be at least one square foot of land above water level year-round and it must support at least two living trees.

The children spend the next while picking one of the small islands and deciding whether it would be suitable to live on. A number of them, being well-acquainted with limited resources, and understanding such things as outhouses and water supplies, argue that most of the small rocky outcrops would not make good places for a cottage or even a tent. In the winter, they would be impossible. These children, many of whose families have had to "make do" for almost everything, likely have a sounder understanding of the basics of survival than many of their more affluent peers.

During the last half hour or so, almost everyone remains seated, the lapping of water against the boat and the afternoon sun streaming through the windows lessening both conversation and activity. Sightseeing has a saturation point, and most of us seem to have reached it. No one is running up and down the aisles, now, and I notice several of my younger students dozing off. Given most of us have been up since five-thirty, it's not any wonder.

The horn sounds, again as we slowly chug to a stop at the Kingston dock. The Captain bids us goodbye and hopes we've had an enjoyable voyage. Everyone tumbles into their bus seat, and, after I stand and do a head count, we head out of the city to Old Fort Henry.

Excitement builds again once the bus draws into a parking lot on one side of the expansive Upper Fort. A guide, in a colourful red and black soldier's uniform, ushers us through a set of side doors into the large open structure and over to the ticket booth. Our school's name produces our ticket package, and I feel a wave of relief knowing everything is in order as Bernadette at Burley Bus Lines said it would be.

We are assigned a guide who begins by telling us his name is Mark and that what we will see is life set in the year of Canada's Confederation, 1867, with men and women doing daily chores of the era. As we pass a guard standing on duty, our guide suggests we should try to make him laugh. Several make faces and dance around him but to no avail. He remains stoically silent.

We are led past an old well in a dry ditch and through a dark archway into the Parade Square of the Lower Fort. David, the mascot goat, parades by, flanked by a soldier in uniform. Rooms where the soldiers lived are small and dark with narrow wooden-framed beds close together. We peek into the cook's kitchen and the wine cellar. Mark leads us down a long, dimly lit tunnel to a room where the cannons were stored. Smells of age-old dampness and oil, combined with seasoned-wood assault us, and I am glad to leave.

He takes us back to a map of the fort and explains that the original Fort Henry was built during the War of 1812 that was fought between 1812 and 1814, and that the fort was strategically located between the Royal Navy dockyards and the St. Lawrence River. "However," Mark goes on, "it bears no resemblance to the existing fort seen on this map."

"What did the original fort look like?" someone asks.

"At the beginning of the War," Mark says, "some local militia erected a blockhouse and battery on the point, here (he points on the map), to defend an important naval base on Point Frederick further west and monitor maritime traffic on the St. Lawrence River and Lake Ontario."

He pauses and asks, "Do you know why this fort was built here?"

Allan shoots up his hand. "During the War of 1812, the British thought the Americans would attack and cut off entry to the trading route at the mouth of the St. Lawrence."

Mark looks pleasantly surprised. I'm not. Allan remembers what I read from the brochure. One of the reasons he always gets top marks in History. "Exactly," the Guide continues, "the loss of this vital trading route would have cut off communication between Kingston and everything east of the city."

"But they didn't attack," someone says, again sounding disappointed.

"There was a slight skirmish," Mark says, smiling. "On November 10th 1812, the battery I mentioned, was involved in a brief clash. They managed to repel several American warships that were attacking the Provincial Marine sloop, Royal George, as the ship was taking refuge in Kingston harbour."

The boys, especially, seem pleased by this addition to the story.

"This naval action," the guide continues, "strengthened the view that a stronger fortification was needed and so the militia and regular army began building the fort you see today."

Mark takes us to a room where dozens of uniforms, hats and swords are stored. Several women in period costumes sit at tables repairing uniforms while a couple of men polish swords.

"We're just in time," he says, leading us back out to the Parade Square. We watch a group of soldiers, using heavy-looking chains, three men to each side, pulling a large gun on wheels. A few minutes later, another group of soldiers marches in formation past us and upstairs to the ramparts, where we see another gun. They load the gun and set it off. The resounding boom makes almost everyone plug their ears, a couple of girls squealing. "War is loud," Mark adds, "loud and foul-smelling."

"I'll say goodbye now," he says, "I hope you enjoyed your tour. Feel free to visit the souvenir shop." He points in its direction. Just then, another group of soldiers appear, marching down the wide cement stairs in perfect rhythm, never missing a step. Mark suggests we march along too. The children line up and try but it's impossible to keep up and, after a few missteps, they laugh and scatter toward the Souvenir shop. The few, who still have cash, buy souvenirs. I purchase a pennant that says "Old Fort Henry."

On the bus trip back, many children and several of the mothers fall asleep. It's been a long and amazing day. We stop at a Trenton truck stop for something to eat, most buying a hamburger and coke, the staff of the not-too-large establishment, scrambling to get all our orders served.

At eight o'clock, when our bus stops in front of the school, a line of tired students files off the bus. Crickets chirp; light is fading and the school stands dark and silent. Most children have someone waiting in a car and those who don't are offered rides. Within five minutes, everyone is gone. I thank our bus driver and climb into the little red Honda, exhausted but still exhilarated. It will be a trip, I hope, many children will remember all their lives.

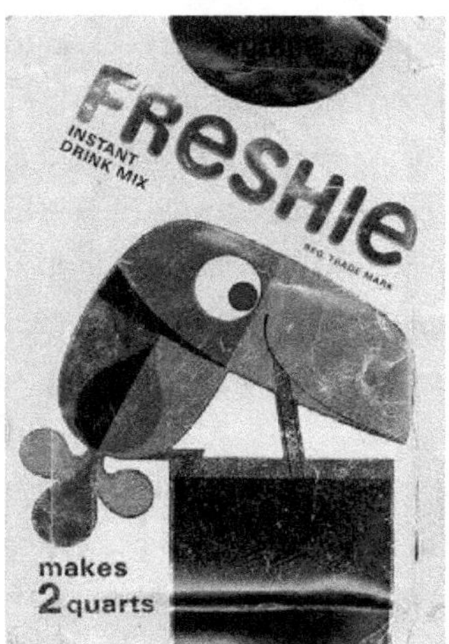

Freshie package

Cleanup Day

On the Monday following the school trip, there's a note on my desk from our janitor, Mrs. Carr:

> Dear Mrs. Manning,
>
> With your permission, I will come to the school first thing this Friday morning for Cleanup Day. We do this every year. The children bring rakes and I bring garbage bags for trash. I also bring Freshie. Younger children can be dismissed early and the older ones will finish.
>
> Mrs. Carr

Following morning exercises, when I mention this to the class, they tell me they do this every year, and that the juniors are dismissed at noon so the seniors can finish the job quickly after lunch. They also tell me they always have a baseball game once cleanup is finished. I don't mention the rakes, as everyone seems to know how the event works.

Thankfully, on Friday, there's a breeze and it's not too hot. Susie, Mrs. Carr's daughter, brings four packets of Freshie in before class, and she and Marilyn prepare two flavours in the jugs we have. Mrs. Carr arrives while we are singing "O Canada" and joins in, a lovely soprano voice. When I ask her if she sings in a choir, she says she wouldn't have time for something like that.

Almost everyone has a rake, and Mrs. Carr supervises the raking crew, setting up several lines of students across the grassy yard. Once a student line has raked grass into a long mound, one of the senior boys appears with a wheelbarrow from the shed, and the grass is gathered up to be dumped by the far fence. The few young ones without rakes are given paper bags and instructed to pick up trash wherever they find it. Some work diligently while others pick up a few pieces and run around chasing each other. I'm not allowed to do anything, and I bring a stack of scribblers out to the front step and sit in the sun, marking.

Half way through the morning, Mrs. Carr announces it's time for a Freshie break. Rakes are leaned up against the school, and everyone files in. Susie and Marilyn pour and hand out drinks in paper cups. As each child is served, he or she sits down in orderly form. I'm so impressed. The whole event carries on beautifully without me. Susie asks me to tell everyone to deposit the paper cups in the waste basket beside the door.

The second half of the morning continues as the first except, by now, the sun is higher and it's getting hot, the yard being without trees. No one complains. When any juniors begin to lag, Mrs. Carr suggests they sit in the shade of the school for a break. I get more marking done than I anticipated and feel quite exhilarated being outside the entire morning.

At a quarter to twelve, several cars pull up, and the drivers call out that they will take anyone home who needs a ride. Juniors bring their paper bags to the steps, surrounding me with varying quantities of trash, some of it smelling decidedly foul. No one complains about handling trash, no matter how putrid, it's simply considered part of the job. I hope they will wash their hands once home and think how I wouldn't let my son, Bruce, pick up rotting material bare-handed, even if he was older.

Again today, I think how lucky these children are, living in this tightly-knit community. The difference and discrimination between well-off and poor families does not extend to needing or not needing a ride. It's simply a common courtesy.

I tell everyone they can bring their lunch outside, and most do. Mrs. Carr and I sit on the front stoop eating ours. She asks me about Bruce, and I say how difficult I find it leaving him every day in spite of the fact Rosamonde and Tante look after him so well. I thank her again for getting the fire going every morning during the cold months. She says her two sons like coming back to the school, now they're in high school, and that they often mention that I'm doing a good job. It's not something I think about, that anyone would be looking over what I'm doing in the school. It reminds me that the School Inspector has not yet made a visit, and I ask Mrs. Carr if she knows who the Inspector is.

"It's probably Mr. Brock, and he'll be showing up one of these days, soon. Likely close to the end of the day. He's near retirement, I understand, and he'll likely want to chat more than inspect."

In the heat of the afternoon, the seniors and a few grade-threes who insisted on staying, finish the raking and make sure every scrap of paper and cigarette package is gone. Mrs. Carr thanks them and hurries off.

Allan and Joe tell me that they are team captains for our baseball game. They take turns choosing players and, in short order, the game begins. I go into the school to mix up the rest of the Freshie and sit at my desk, listening to the cheering, egging on, and groaning when the ball is missed.

By the ninth inning, everyone is beginning to flag. Balls are missed both by batters and fielders, and the score is fifteen-twelve in favour of

Allan's team. Everyone comes in for a final drink before leaving.. When Marilyn and Susie say they'll stay to clean up, I insist I will look after it. They both look tired but protest only half-heartedly. I shoo them out and get on with it. These country children certainly know how to pitch in and get work done. When I leave, the yard looks pristine and tidy. I glance at the peeling paint on school bricks and window ledges and wish someone could have a go at them too, but I also know it's not going to happen.

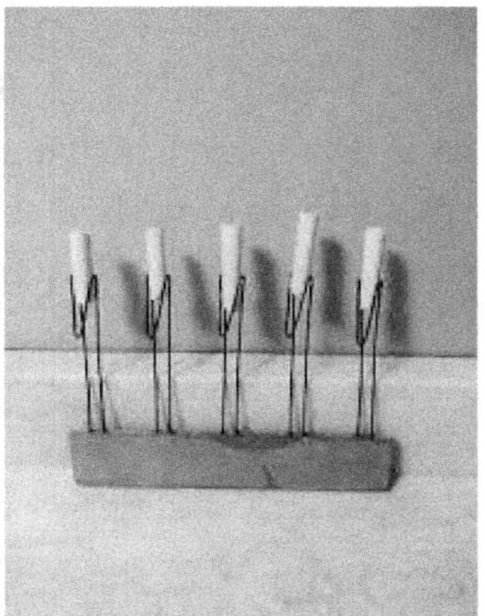

Chalk holder for staff lines

Music Challenge and The Inspector

On June 3rd, two days before our school trip, Mr. Thrip had announced to the seniors that he would be teaching a song in the minor key and that they must review the major key signatures and their relative minors. Up until this point in the school year, he has never mentioned the minor key, and I am somewhat alarmed. I have no idea what was taught in previous years, and only one or two of the senior students seem to know anything about this music term. When they faltered over several of the questions he asked, Mr. Thrip looked somewhat apologetic and said that grades five to eight must know all minor key signatures for the music exam on June twenty-fourth. He added that as there wasn't much time left, everyone should do the best they could. He went through all the key signatures, but I could tell most of my students were lost. When the lesson was over, he quietly said to me that his teaching time-line was more challenging in a one-room school, but he hoped the children could rise to the occasion. I nodded and vowed, silently, that we most certainly would.

I have less than three weeks to review all subjects leading up to exams which I have decided will begin June 18th and end on the 23rd. I'm going to use multiple-choice again and have already begun work on them. I have not planned to start a crash course in music theory at this late date. However, this is exactly what I do.

First thing every afternoon, during silent reading time, I drill the major keys and their relative minors. The following morning, along with our regular work, I put five major key signatures on the blackboard and ask the seniors to find its relative minor and write the matching scale. Several students tell me that the teacher before me felt music was Mr. Thrip's job and did little review during the week. I'm sure he had as little time as I do to work on this, however, after one week of drilling, I see some improvement.

The school inspector arrives Tuesday the following week, about a half hour before dismissal. I hear the door open and shut, and turn from writing on the board to see a man dressed in a suit, his tie pulled loose. "I'm Mr. Brock," he calls out, "your inspector. Just carry on." I know I should be nervous but, this late in the day I'm too preoccupied with getting things finished.

The grade one's and two's are looking at their readers, supposedly practising what silent reading they can manage; grades three and four are finishing a science assignment; grades five and six are working on history questions from the board, and my grade sevens are looking at a map of the world, finding locations needed in a geography project.

The room is quiet except for grade seven's whispering, and I look around at the filled blackboards, a few pencils and papers scattered on the floor, the sun coming through the west window, highlighting a shaft of dust. It's not tidy here, but I hope it looks as though we are busy.

Mr. Thrip will be here tomorrow, and I want to go over the major minor keys posted on the board one more time. I'm not sure if going over music is substantial enough for the inspector or whether he would want me to be doing math or history. He seems to be pleased, walking up and down the aisles, asking questions and inspecting scribblers. I decide I will do what I intended.

"We are expecting Mr. Thrip, the music teacher, tomorrow," I say to Mr. Brock. "We're perfecting the relative major and minor keys."

He looks up and nods. "You go ahead and do whatever is it is you would always do. I'll stand at the back out of your way."

I tell the seniors to put away the books they're not taking home for exam prep and add that the juniors who want to listen in are welcome to do so. I have a chart on the west blackboard:

Key signatureMajor KeyMinor Key
F#G majorE minor
F#, C#D majorB minor
F#, C#, G#A majorF# minor

I cover the major key list with a large piece of bristol board and ask students to name each major, followed by each minor that goes with the visible key list. Everything goes smoothly, correct answers given for each set of keys. Mr. Brock nods and looks pleased as we continue.

I ask Marilyn to draw, on the board, three sets of staff lines and with treble clefs, and hand her the chalk holder. I pause momentarily, hoping my next request will result in correct answers. Three students accurately produce three relative minor scales. It's clear they've almost nailed it, at least some of them have.

I whisper to my two blackboard monitors that, if possible, could they arrive early tomorrow morning? I'm sure the inspector will want to talk with no one else around. Thankfully, both agree to be at the school by 7:30 A.M.

I remind everyone about studying for exams and announce dismissal. My students know the inspector is an important person, and

I'm grateful that they file out in an unusually quiet and orderly fashion, probably feeling a little intimidated, but unaware that I am being graded.

After they leave, Mr. Brock pulls up a chair adjacent to my desk and chews the fat, as Mrs. Carr had projected. He complains about the long distances between schools; the lack of personal hygiene in some schools, and hints at lack of discipline and shoddy teacher preparation. "You seem to be doing very well," he says, with a sweep of his hand around the room. "Doesn't look like you have any discipline problems."

"I was very strict the first few weeks. But now, we're more like a large family."

"So no problems, so far?"

"I do have one situation I'm not sure how to deal with," I say. I pause, wanting to ask about the Stoaker children being absent over two thirds of the year.

He nods and looks thoughtful. "Would it be the two Stoaker children?" he asks.

"You know about them?" I immediately realize, of course, he would, as they've been a concern for years. "Right now, it's exams I'm worried about, and their report cards."

"Just give them a letter grade," he says, shaking his head. "It's the same every year. I have more like them in several other schools."

"I have tried to give them extra help when they show up. But they're so far behind, and the older one really isn't interested."

"It's one of the hazards of a country school. And if they're needed at home on the farm, there's not much you can do."

I don't mention their lack of personal hygiene or their obvious lack of proper nutrition. There's not much he could do either. After a pause, I add, "I am enjoying teaching here."

"In spite of the work load?"

"I still spend two or three hours every evening, marking mostly. And eight to ten hours on the weekend."

"You do take some time off, I hope?"

"I have a young son being looked after by my mother-in-law and, yes, I do spend as much time as possible with him."

"And your husband?"

"Away working." I refrain from elaborating, and he doesn't ask.

He stands and extends his hand. "It's been a pleasure," he says, shaking mine. "Carry on. You're doing fine." And he's gone, out the door, his car door slamming, the sound of his vehicle driving off. I sit, shaking, wondering if I've said and done the right things. No one prepared me for this, and I had no idea what to expect.

A couple of weeks later, I receive two letters in the mail: invitations to teach at two Cobourg schools. I'm more than surprised and wonder why they would be doing this, not realizing, at the time, that my reputation has preceded me. I do know I will be leaving at the end of the 1965 school year, when I have earned my Permanent Certificate. I don't know, as yet, what I will be doing. My husband's job contract will come to an end in May, and he's looking for work in Toronto. We won't be staying here, that I know. Would I go and teach in a town school next year with its better pay, with only one or two grades at the most? I know the answer instantly. No. I will stay with these children, my children. The older ones, especially, have had a series of teachers, several not too competent from what they've told me, and now, given I've survived my first year, why would I want to go anywhere else? I handwrite two polite replies stating simply that I intend to stay at the Front Road School West for another year.

It's only a few days later that my Board member, Mr. Moore, tells me that next year will be the final year for the school, that the children will be split up and moved to other graded rural schools. This is an added reason to stay, to give these children the best last year here. It will be difficult especially for the younger ones who have always had older siblings in the classroom and on the playground. Although I plan not to break this news to everyone until our last day, I suspect some of the older ones know already.

Final Exams

The two weeks prior to exams are a whirlwind of review, with me hoping everyone will do well and pass to the next grade. After each exam, I stay up well past midnight, marking. I continue to drill the seniors with daily quizzes using the major and minor keys. They're good-natured about it, and many have improved substantially. I find the children to be amazingly reasonable when asked to learn specifics in a certain subject. This is still the era of teacher supremacy, and I have tried to be reasonable—until now. Now I've become determined everyone will have enough knowledge of the minor keys to impress Mr. Thrip. I think their co-operation and patience with me, labouring day after day over quizzes, confirms this, even though I'm not aware of it at the time. I've promised report cards for the last day of school which will give me one day to enter music marks.

The day after our last exam, Mr. Thrip arrives with a final test prepared. I have told the juniors to try and be quiet outside as this exam is important. He has everyone clear their desks except for a pen or pencil and says they will have exactly forty-five minutes. He places a test, faced downwards on each desk, walks slowly to the front, and says they may turn their papers over and begin. I find this protocol interesting as I am substantially more relaxed in my exam routine. I do remember this approach from high school, however.

The test is multiple-choice, and I'm glad the children are now familiar with this format. The room is the quietest it has been in his presence. I look over the questions and am so glad I've worked on the major and minor keys. A quarter of the exam is given to this part of the music course. At forty minutes, he cautions that only five minutes are left. Only a couple of students are still finishing and most sit looking out the window, a few with their heads down, resting. Even with the windows open, it's already hot in the school.

I'm surprised and relieved that he has the students exchange papers so the marking can be done right away. Once finished, he gathers up the papers and asks to sit in my desk to tally the results. I dismiss the seniors and follow them outside. They stand in groups discussing the questions, some groaning, and some saying how easy it was. After a few minutes, they disperse to play baseball, skip, or bounce balls against the side of the school. The little ones flock around me asking when they can go inside. Even though the sun is beating down, no one wears hats or suntan lotion. Its detrimental effects are unheard of in the 1960's.

After about twenty minutes, I wander back inside and begin tidying up the back table, thinking I should take all the dishes home for a good wash.

"Mrs. Manning?"

I turn to see him putting the exam papers into a large manila envelope.

"I have the marks here for you to enter into your report cards."

"How did my students do?"

He hands me the results on a piece of paper. "Much better than I expected. I can tell you've been drilling them. I appreciate that."

"I learned along with them. They're such a good bunch of kids."

"Not everyone takes to a one room school." He closes his briefcase. "It's obvious you have. Hope your summer goes well." He smiles briefly and is gone.

The report has letter grades already listed for the juniors, and it appears that this exam mark is the one each senior will receive, that no earlier tests or class participation are included. The marks are better than I expected. I resolve that, next year, we'll start working on the minor keys in January not June.

The children wait until the car has driven off to flock in and ask about their marks. Once everyone is seated, I say the marks are better than either I or Mr. Thrip anticipated and that no one failed. "Report cards tomorrow," I say, smiling. "You'll just have to wait." There are groans and nods, and one of the grade-three students says that tomorrow is such a long time away.

By now, it's nearly dismissal time and I decide to let everyone go fifteen minutes early. It's one of those hot June days and the school room, even with the windows open, is humid and uncomfortable. After dismissal, I stand for a few minutes on the front step watching them traipse off in both directions, arms swinging, some running in short bursts, a few of the older boys jostling each other. One more day, and I'll be free for the entire summer.

All I have to do now is enter the music marks into the report cards. This reminds me of the Stoaker children and what to do if they don't show up tomorrow. Given they have not been at school for over a month and have missed exams, I know I will have to fail both of them. Since talking to the inspector, I'm not as worried as to how this will reflect on my teaching, but I still haven't put the damning letter marks into their report cards. Everyone agrees there is nothing that can be done about them. Part of me thinks how wrong it is to simply write them off as if they don't matter. I wonder about Gerald, who at thirteen is still in grade five and, as his mother told me in the fall, will not be returning to school. I know the Inspector's comment about them being needed on the farm is valid, but I'm fairly sure these children will have a hard time in life, even in this small town community. I've asked Mr. Moore and even mentioned it to Rosamonde and Tante, but I never get a remotely satisfactory answer. I have so much to do, day to day, that it's only at times like this that I think about them and feel guilty wishing I could help. These children are so unequipped to deal with life after they leave; most of them likely won't make it to high school. It's not your problem, I say fiercely to myself; concentrate on everyone else. By now, the road is empty with only the occasional car driving by and, once inside, I check the thermometer on the back wall; it's eighty-one degrees Fahrenheit, time to lock up and call it a day.

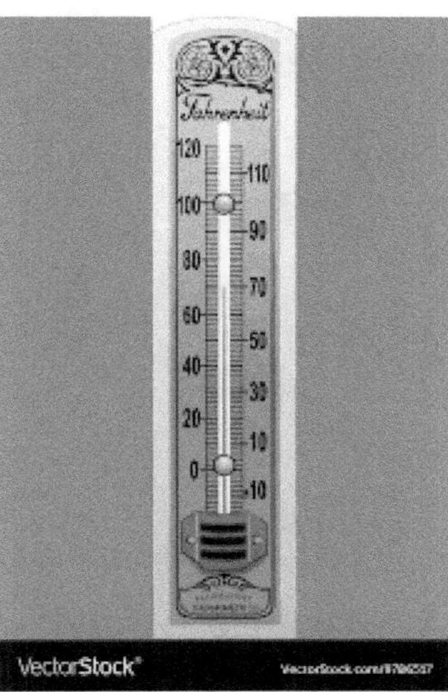

Fahrenheit thermomenter

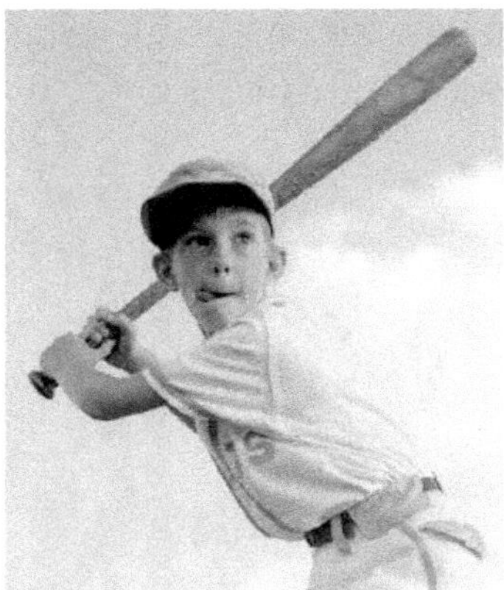

Boy batting

Last Day before Holidays

I arrive early on the last day so I can make sure all report cards are in order by grade. Mrs. Carr has already cleaned and washed the blackboards, as well as all the window ledges. Many of the children have taken most of their books and scribblers home, and desks already have an empty look. Last week, I bundled up the record player and most of the books I brought. I didn't think to write down titles and have no idea if the books are all here or if one or two are at someone's house. I did keep the novel we have not quite finished, and plan to read to the end this morning.

It's always much cooler first thing in the morning, the trees along the creek casting long shadows against the school's east wall, that damp dew smell drifting in through the windows. I walk around the room with mixed feelings. On one hand, I'm thankful the school year is over. I'll have endless time to spend with Bruce. Jim will be back permanently early in May and we'll be a family again. On the other hand, I know I will miss everyone: the daily routine I'm so accustomed to, the unexpected things that happen, even the traumas.

This musing comes to an end when the door opens. I expect it to be one of the regulars and am surprised to see Gerald Stoaker, baseball cap in hand, looking somewhat tentative.

"Come in, Gerald," I say, "I'm glad you're here today."

He stops by the stove, his beanpole frame silhouetted against the black vertical pipe. "I've come to get the report cards," he says, his bass voice distinctly that of a man's.   "Essie's still at home."

"Your report cards are right here." I sort through the pile to find them. He approaches slowly, head slightly bent and takes them from me, looking somewhat embarrassed.

"Thanks," he mutters, and hurries toward the door. "Got to get back home."

"Have a good summer," I call out, feeling immediately that this is a ridiculous thing to say, that he's probably glad to be rid of school. Who knows how his summer will go, how any of the Stoaker children will make out? Will there be enough food? Does their father ever come home? I know there's a baby, a girl who has a hole in her heart and has spent a good deal of her short life at Sick Children's Hospital. The entire situation seems fraught with problems, but, as I tell myself again, there's nothing I can do.

Soon afterwards, several of the senior girls come in and place wrapped gifts on my desk, giggling as they do so. They rush out before I can think of what to say. I wasn't expecting anything and it makes me momentarily teary. Several more gifts appear a few minutes later, and a card signed by everyone.

At nine, I ring the bell, and everyone piles in, not as quietly as usual. For once, I don't care. As soon as Opening Exercises are over, I tell them I will give out Report Cards before lunch and that we'll have our last baseball game in the afternoon.

Two or three hands shoot up and someone blurts out, "Are you going to open your gifts?"

"You want me to open them now?"

"Yes, yes," everyone chants, some even clapping. And so I open these gifts: a set of homemade pot holders, a small vase, a brooch the shape of a rose, a silky-feeling scarf with bluebirds on it, several candy bars, and the card with almost everyone's signature squeezed inside and on the back. I admire each item and thank everyone. I look at the time; it's only nine forty-five.

I'm planning on having an art session and story reading session, but before I have time to explain, a hand shoots up to ask if I will read from the Gulliver book.

"This is part of my plan for this morning," I say. "I will read to you, and you will draw pictures about what is going on in the story."

A junior hand is up. "I already took my crayons home."

"I am hoping you will use your pencil and take it home to colour."

Everyone nods, getting out their pencils, even the little ones. A few, of course, need to visit the pencil sharpener. Before I came up with this idea, I was at a loss to know what to do on this last day, regular lessons being out of the question. A couple of the older children pass out paper, and I begin to read. Time disappears, and pencils are furiously drawing. By eleven-thirty, I read the last lines. There is a cumulative sigh.

"Will you be here next year?" one of the grade two students asks.

"Yes, I will," I say.

"And you'll read us another Gulliver?" another chimes in.

"I think there may be another story," I reply. "If not, I'll find something just as good."

Most students, knowing it's nearly lunch time, tuck their art work in their desks.

I shuffle the stack of report cards, and as I stand, everyone becomes absolutely quiet. "I have an announcement to make before I hand out report cards." I hear a couple of students catch their breaths and I know some are worried about failing. "This has nothing to do with your marks, and I know as some of you have likely heard rumours. It's official so I can tell you. Our next year together will be the last year this school will be open."

"But where will we go?" someone asks.

"Will we still all be together?" another voice chimes in.

"I don't have any answers yet," I say, "but I'm sure I'll be able to give you more information in the fall." I know some of the children will be upset and decide the best way to deal with it would be to get at the task at hand. "I would like to give out your report cards," I say before anyone else has a hand up. The room is silent again. I can barely hear anyone breathing.

"I want to say," I begin, "that no one present has failed this year." A rush of sighs drifts into one and there is relief on a number of faces. "However," I add, "I will expect some of you to do better next year." I call out each name, in turn, beginning with the grade sevens. The stillness, except for the footfall of each one receiving a card, continues. Once all are distributed, older siblings check out younger ones' grades, and everyone relaxes again.

I have thought about suggesting we eat outside, a picnic on the last day, but as there is not enough shade, and as heat is pouring in the windows on both sides, I announce it's lunchtime and take out my lunch prepared by Rosamonde. On the one hand, I know I am spoiled being so well looked after by my husband's mother and aunt while, on the other hand, I've been so busy I haven't had much time to think about it. Until now. How many lunches have they prepared for me, and how many dinners? I know Bruce is getting to be a handful for them and I am already thinking about alternatives for next fall, someone who could babysit him, perhaps.

My musings are interrupted by Allan and Joe who come forward to ask when they can pick teams. I suggest they go outside for fifteen minutes. I will come out then and we can begin. I know they will, informally, have the teams figured out before I'm there; even the little ones will be on one team or the other. This only happens on special occasions, the previous one being on Cleanup Day. Usually, an older child helps hold the bat for the younger one and the pitcher moves closer, throwing a gentle ball. Most of the time, whoever it is, is out on first base. But there are always surprises.

It's a hot afternoon, and by two o'clock everyone has had enough. We go back inside so that desks can be cleared, all belongings to be taken home. Almost everyone collects up their art work, and I have a few spare plastic bags for those who lament that they can't carry everything. At two-thirty, I bid them all a good summer and stand by the door as they file out.

It takes a while as almost everyone gives me a hug, and I have a hard time holding back tears. I watch them scatter in both directions, on bicycles, walking, skipping, running, many of them whooping and cheering. For some, it will be freedom for two whole months, for others added farm chores and more responsibility. I smile as I watch a breeze tumble several pieces of art work across the road and school yard.

My first year of teaching is over. I really am a teacher now.

I take one last look inside the school. The pit toilets are now in dire need of cleaning, and I shudder to think who has to do it. With gifts and other paraphernalia, it takes three trips to my little car to get everything gathered up. I know Mrs. Carr will be there to put the place back into the pristine condition it was when I first visited almost a year ago. I open all my car windows, batten down anything that might blow away, and drive off.

Next year will be the last one for this hundred-year-old schoolhouse, and I plan to make it the best year possible.

Year Two: 1964 – 1965

"You don't remember what happened. What you remember becomes what happened."
John Green *An Abundance of Katherines*

"Memory fades, memory adjusts, memory conforms to what we think we remember."
Joan Didion *Blue Nights*

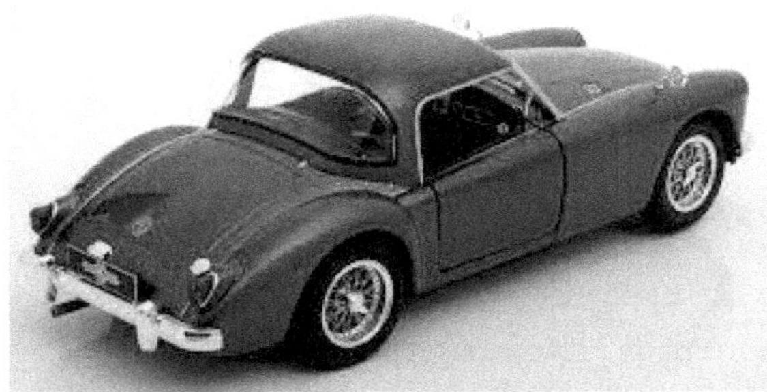

MGA sports car

Fall 1964

Summer seems endless during July, but once August begins I'm again thinking of school, the curriculum, and my students. I'll have eight grades this year. I find out in mid-August that there will be four new students in grade one. Starting mid-month, I spend weekday mornings at the school getting courses ready. I must set up courses for the grade eights and, since last year, I taught the grade five and seven courses in history, geography and science, this year grades five and six will take the grade six courses, and grades seven and eight will take the grade eight curriculum. Thankfully, because I now know what will work and what won't, I'm faster and more efficient.

Since his Burrough's computer installation contract ended in May, Jim is back in Cobourg and has been working for the United Counties of Northumberland Durham as a Survey Crew Chief. He's still looking for a computer-related job, and his sights are set on Toronto, as there's nothing in the Cobourg area.

In mid-August, Jim announces that someone on the survey crew is selling their 1957 hardtop MGA and, a few weeks later, it belongs to us.

We had both decided that, even though Rosamonde drives her red Honda infrequently, I should have my own car in the fall. I have no feeling for cars and, even though the MG is considerably more exotic than our much newer Austin, I'm fine with the idea of driving it. Jim says it won't be practical for him to commute with the MG to a Toronto job but, in the meantime, he wants to drive it.

Since mid-August, Bruce has been attending half-days at Mrs. Cable's day care in Cobourg. She has preschool children and, along with Bruce, several others arrive each day. Bruce was, of course, initially nervous and not too pleased the first day, hanging on to my hand when I went to leave, begging that he leave with me. It only took a couple of days, though, before he was ready before I was, running to get in the car and be off to see his friends. Often, when I went to pick him up those weekdays in August, he would beg me to stay longer and luckily, the transition from half to full days has been an extremely positive one.

Over the summer I, again, begin thinking about taking a university course. I wanted so much to attend university after high school but there was no money to do this. Then, confident I was destined for a stage career, I took the advice of my school principal and applied to Ryerson Institute to take Radio and Television Arts. There were no post-secondary theatre arts courses in those days, and the course overview contained the following: "The secondary school graduate whose interests include literature, public speaking, music, dramatics, and who possesses initiative, originality, and the ability to work hard, is most likely to succeed in this course." This seemed perfect to me at nineteen and I ignored any of the technical course descriptions. RTA did not turn out to be a program I enjoyed; rather I endured it and skipped a lot of classes. The courses focussed on becoming someone versed in the technical aspects of the radio and television industry, neither of which interested me in the least, and the arts courses seemed to be diminished versions of what my friends were taking at university. By cramming over the last month, I managed to pass all courses, having already decided I would not return in the fall. Instead, I made a hundred and eighty degree turn in my life by marrying and attending Teacher's College. My parents were, understandably, not happy with my decision to marry at such a young age. Jim and I deliberately waited until after my twentieth birthday for our wedding ceremony, so that I would no longer be a teenager.

I decided on Teacher's College as a way to appease my mother who felt I was throwing my life away and would have no adequate training should I need to work sometime in the future. I endured and completed the one year course which turned out to be far more tedious and demoralizing than Ryerson. I knew my path was not following society's rules and my response was to throw caution to the wind and carry on.

Now, of course it has paid off and so, again in 1964, I begin dreaming of a university degree. That I am teaching eight grades and have a young son, does not deter me. After discussing my options with Jim, I sign up for Introductory Psychology, a correspondence course through Queen's University.

The first day of school, in September, is considerably different from a year ago. For starters, I'm driving a sporty little MG with leather seats and wooden trim. Jim, who is driving our Austin, looks longingly at the MG and says he hopes I'll enjoy driving it. I soon love it: folding myself into the leather seat, changing gears, feeling the road beneath me; I'm hooked after driving it once. I know my students will notice and wonder if any will comment.

I arrive at school early, before anyone else, this small room cramped with too many desks welcoming me: the stove shining and clean, the blackboards pristine with new chalk already placed strategically along the troughs thanks to Mrs. Carr, the windows open slightly, the morning air fresh. I check one last time that the new seating arrangements, I set up several weeks ago, are in order. This new seating plan, moves the new grade fives to the larger desks and I am relieved to have the right-sized desks for each grade. I'm sure if I didn't I would be told to 'make do', the standard response to most requests last year.

Today, as students begin arriving, each comes in to say hello and ask me how my summer was. I can see through the open front door that several of the older boys are clustered around my car but when they come in to say hello, they don't comment on it. I assume they feel it would be presumptuous and make a mental note to mention it before classes begin.

My four new grade-ones, each looking more than a little apprehensive, arrive with an older sibling. None of these children says anything beyond parroting the "Good morning" of their brother or sister, all of them staring resolutely at the floor. I suggest, in order to ease their anxiety, that their sibling give them a tour of the room. The stove and toilets garner the most attention. As each duo completes the tour, I point out their individual desks, each designated with their name printed on a piece of lined printing paper. This instant ownership pleases each one and they sit, inspecting the ink bottle hole and the shallow pencil trough. The drawer is opened and closed several times, just to make sure it works.

When I step out to ring the bell, everyone rushes into line, the few who haven't already greeted me, doing so. "Good morning," I say before I usher them inside, "good to see all of you again." I point to my car. "You may have noticed I have a different car," I say casually. "It's an MG my husband bought second-hand over the summer." A cumulative "ahh" ensues, and everyone turns to look.

I found out when interviewing former students for this book that this car was the most talked about item for the first few weeks of school. Some of the boys were sure it was for racing and thought, on weekends, that's what we were likely doing.

On this first morning in September, almost everyone finds their last year's seat, with those moving up to senior status taking the more prestigious desks and chairs. Cathy Burnham, now in grade five, has brought a book containing music for *God Save the Queen* which begins with an impressive eight bar intro. As we're singing, many more in tune than this time last year, I'm thinking that last year's music program did improve things and promise myself that this year we'll be even better.

Although there have been some unusually warm days once we're into October, most nights and early mornings are damp and crisp. Probably because I'm under considerably less stress than I was this time last year, I notice things that, previously, slipped by me. One of these is the fact that a number of my students bring less than adequate lunches: a jam sandwich on white bread or just a few store-bought cookies. It's no wonder these children are pale and lagging by mid-afternoon. It seems obvious to me, now, that this is likely the main reason they don't do as well as their better-fed classmates.

Thinking that a more nutritious lunch will engender more productively through the afternoon, I decide I will set up a lunchtime soup program, and that it will be free with the option of a donation. I have no idea whether or not my students will find this useful or appropriate, but I'm going to give it a try. I know from my Teachers' College days that inner city schools in economically depressed areas of Toronto have lunchtime soup programs and reason that my school population represents a microcosm of this situation.

Before I mention this plan to my students, I cut and paste construction paper over last year's Red Cross donation box. I'm hoping children from more affluent families will make donations, and, if there isn't enough money in a given week, I will supplement from my income. I do think of asking my Board member, Mr. Moore, for a donation, but know, if I do, it could take weeks before I get an answer which could easily be 'no.' When I send notes to student homes about the program, he will be aware of it anyway.

I talk it over, first, with my three grade seven and eight girls who think it's a great idea and want to help set the program in place. After discussing different kinds and packaging of soups available, we settle on Lipton dried soup mix, it being easy to prepare and generous in portions. The girls say chicken noodle and tomato vegetable will be the most popular. It doesn't occur to me that initiating the program is innovative; it is simply something I think needs to be done. On Friday, before dismissal, I announce to the class that, beginning on Monday and continuing as long as needed, a Soup-for-lunch program will begin and that those who want to participate should bring a mug and spoon. I emphasize that having soup at lunchtime will benefit everyone and that to fund this program, I will ask for donations from those who can help out financially. I also show them the newly-minted Soup Collection Box, saying I will put five dollars in to get things started.

Rosamonde and Tante are enthusiastic about my plan and, over the weekend, they help me find a good-sized spare pot, as well as a large wooden spoon and ladle. Bruce and I always go grocery shopping on Saturdays, and, when I mention that we're going to have Lipton's soup at lunchtime in my school, he tells me that at Mrs. Cable's they have Lipton's soup almost every day.

This comment twinges my conscience, and, as I am picking cans and boxes and produce from shelves, and Bruce is happily chattering, I again work through my 'working mother' guilt. The sixties are still a period when mothers are expected to stay home, and magazine articles are written about the potential damage done if this is not the case. Even though, for a few minutes after dropping him off each day, I feel acute separation anxiety, I know he's happy being there, playing and interacting with other children his age. It's an ongoing tug-of-war between my heart and head.

When I arrive at school Monday morning and count how many children want soup, I find fifteen have brought mugs and spoons. I have wisely brought a half a dozen more, knowing some, likely those who need it the most, will have forgotten. Susie and Marilyn have made room on the back table for the mugs and say that they will make the soup each day for this week.

I make a chart for "Soup and Wash Up Monitors" and encourage older students to sign up for the job. It carries a crucial aspect of responsibility, entailing being sure to watch the time in order to prepare the soup to be ready for noon. These monitors must: bring the measured water to a boil, add the dried soup mix, stir and make sure there are no lumps, and have the hot soup ready by twelve. After lunch is over and most of the children have gone outside, these students must heat more water to wash the mugs, spoons, and soup kettle.

By the end of the first week, I realize I should bring more dish detergent and several extra tea towels. We set up a small clothes line to hang them on. Although the soup is not expensive, I'm pleased that the "Soup Box" usually has enough cash to cover the next week's allotment. Soon, almost everyone is having soup at lunch, and I'm fairly sure the more affluent children are providing most of the needed cash.

I decide I'll continue the program until May when the hot weather will make soup less desirable. I repeatedly spend time during Health class, held once a week for all grades, to talk about what should be included in a packed lunch. Children who already bring an adequate lunch are always quick to tell me the essential components while those whose meals are lacking, either stare at their desks or look worried. Again, as with the Stoaker children, I wish I could help but I can't. This soup program will have to suffice.

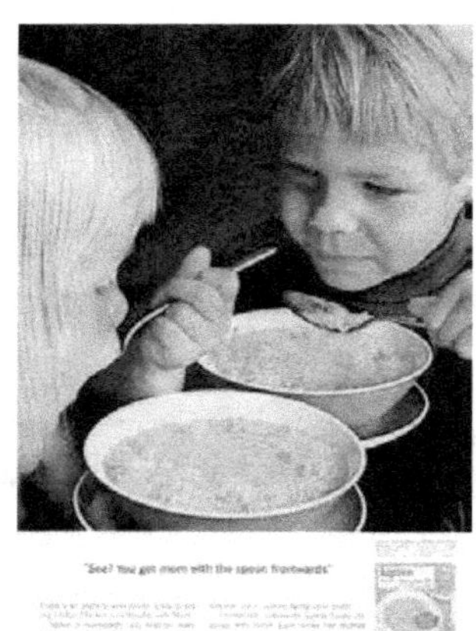

The soup program

Christmas Concert and New Subjects

By the mid-November, I've received word that my students will be split up and sent to a number of area schools and that bussing is a likelihood. I also know that for the grade eights the transition into high school will be a huge disruption. In 1954, my terror of starting grade nine after three years in one room at the Baltimore school is still clear. I'm sure most of my students will not have to walk two and a half miles to get the bus as I did, but they will have to wait in all kinds of weather, and the first few weeks will be stressful.

Added to this is the fact that those going into grade nine and possibly grade eight will be expected to have had experience in subjects they have never taken, specifically home economics, industrial arts called shop, and physical education. I decide, therefore, that in the New Year, even though it will be a challenge, I will have courses set in place for grades five to eight in each of these subjects.

Things are running smoothly this fall term, and I find that a number of older children have often finished their day's work by mid-afternoon or earlier. The week after exams in November, I spend several sessions before dismissal, telling the children what I want to do concerning these new subjects and asking for suggestions that will help set the plan in motion. Everyone agrees that beginning these classes in January is most practical as, once the weather turns nasty, being inside for any activity is more appealing. We decide that, beginning the first week in January following afternoon recess, those in grades six and up who have finished their day's work will work on a home economics known as home ec or an industrial arts/shop project on a rotating basis, and that we will introduce physical education or physed at the beginning of February.

Several suggest that we could even work on these projects at noon hour and during afternoon recess as well.

Beginning the first week in December, this discussion is forgotten and all extra attention focuses on the Christmas concert. An unspoken determination and fervour surround each task: the boys, again, bring in the Christmas tree, the tree is decorated, sheet curtains brought in for the show, the platform brought in and assembled. It's clear everyone wants this to be the best concert ever for our little school. Backdrops are more elaborate; I find a more suitable play with speaking parts and, best of all, by asking Mr. Thrip well in advance, manage to get copies of the music we will be presenting. Cathy Burnham offers to go over the melody line of all the pieces, and, after several extra rehearsals at noon hour and afternoon recess, everyone performs their songs with more confidence. We even get positive comments from Mr. Thrip.

The concert goes off without a hitch and one of the highlights is a duet by grade two students Linda Burnham and Carol-Ann Hoselton singing "All I Want for Christmas is My Two Front Teeth." Linda has these teeth missing and as the song ends, the entire audience is on its feet, whistling and clapping; another Kodak moment left unrecorded.

As with last year, Santa makes a visit to distribute gifts, and it's always magical to see the younger students' awe-struck faces, especially the grade-ones for whom this experience is a first. Treats, drinks, and conversation round out the evening. After everyone has left, I feel an overwhelming sense of endings, for me, for the children, and for this tired old building.

I wonder, as I lock the door, whether anyone will buy the place; try to live here. So many upgrades would be needed to make it habitable even for one person. The children and I, at this point, take as normal the pit toilets, the stained sink with its cold water tap, the wind and snow coming in through windows during the winter months. Even though almost all of them live in houses equipped with the expected amenities, for most students especially in the senior grades, this is all they've ever known or expected at school.

January will bring its own set of challenges, one of which will be logistics surrounding the three new courses I plan to introduce. Nineteen sixty-five will be a year of exciting new beginnings layered with inevitable and emotional endings.

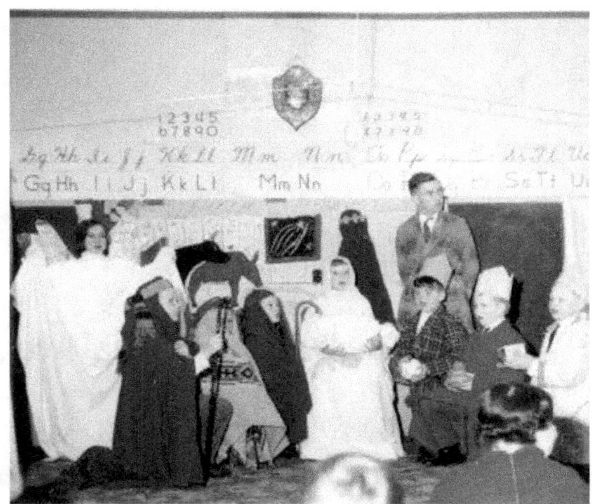

Xmas Concert 1964

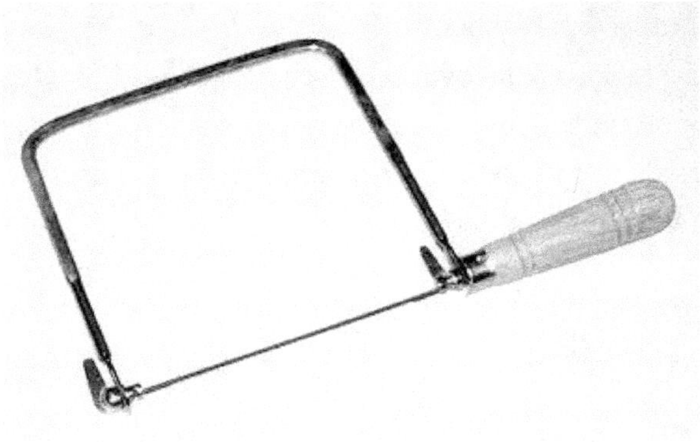

Coping saw

Home Economics and Industrial Arts

The first day back to school in January is cold with only a minimal amount of snow on the ground. The children pile in, all seemingly eager to be back. Immediately after opening exercises, several hands shoot up and questions begin. "When will we start home ec and shop?" "What will we do in each of these subjects?"

I have given some thought to this over the holidays and tell the class that I have purchased, through The Cobourg Book Store, a book called *How to Use a Coping Saw*. In it, are instructions for building a bird house. This we will use for the shop course. I go on to say I plan to bring my portable Singer sewing machine and have found a pattern for making an apron. We will begin these classes a week from today. In the meantime, I ask students who are participating to search at home pieces of wood for the bird house and a yard of suitable material for the apron.

During the week, wood and material appear, some of it useful, some not. I bring the sewing machine and set it up on one of two empty desks at the back of the room. Realizing that we will need a large surface for laying out material and for cutting the pinned pattern, I find the stored card table we were given as a wedding present and bring it to school. When I mention I'm not sure how we will manage the sawing of wood, the Wilson boys bring in a rough but serviceable bench.

We move desks forward to make room for these two items. With wood piled in the back corner and pieces of material stacked in brown paper bags under the sink, our one-room has become even more cluttered than usual. By the end of the week, all the boys have brought pieces of wood, and all but one of the girls, material for an apron. To ensure everyone has enough suitable wood and material, I announce that I will bring extra wood and several more pieces of material in case anyone needs them. I have asked Rosamonde and Tante who have pulled a number of suitable material ends and pieces from various cupboards and drawers. Bruce and I have also looked inside the shed attached to the Manning garage where decades of wood, discarded furniture, and other castoffs lie coated in dust and age. We have found quite a collection of suitable wood lengths which Jim and Bruce have deposited into the trunk of our Austin.

From our bedroom storage cupboard I've located the equipped sewing basket given to me by my grandmother as a wedding present. I know she, now in her nineties, is pleased I am teaching, as she began her working career as a teacher at age seventeen in Churubusco Public School, Indiana, USA. In 1901, in her second year of teaching, she had sixty-four students in a grade two/three class. I can only imagine the effort involved in working with this large a number of young children.

I have not used this sewing basket since making maternity clothes and am delighted to rediscover two pairs of scissors, a measuring tape, thread, pins, and a pin cushion, as well as extra bobbins for the sewing machine.

On Monday afternoon, I spend an inordinate amount of time helping the first two hopefuls work on their projects. I know nothing about making a bird house, however, and I am relieved to find out that the Wilson brothers and Joe Harper have made things with wood and are competent and willing to help those who have not. I am, however, fairly adept at sewing.

Before my teaching days, during the first winter after Teacher's College, when we moved to Senneterre, Quebec, Jim bought me the sewing machine I've brought to school. With almost no sewing experience beyond a dismal experience of making a much-too-large-blouse in my high school home economics class, I decided to sew maternity smocks and dresses. The early 1960s were still the days when maternity clothes were mandatory, dresses one wore as soon as one began to "show." I chose a difficult Vogue dress pattern with bound button holes, and, needless to say, it provided me with a formidable challenge and much frustration.

An apron, on the other hand, will be straight forward and easy. I do not anticipate, however, that some students will have extreme difficulty pinning the pattern on the material and cutting it out. Tears ensue several times when pieces of material are either cut crumpled, mistakenly pinned on the bias, pinned over the edge of the material, or cut before I have a chance to check them. I'm glad I have brought extra material. I stress that making mistakes is part of the learning process and that, when the apron is finished, there will be a sense of accomplishment. The boys do not seem to have as many problems, although I notice wood that must have been miss-cut, tossed into the wood bin.

I find the noise from the sewing machine and sawing/nailing a distraction. Most students, however, seem to be able to ignore it. After several of the younger ones keep asking if they can watch, I relent, saying once their day's work is complete and corrected, a maximum of three students may watch at each project. I stress that they must stand back so as not to interfere, and not ask questions. Most who go to watch, last only a few minutes, but there are a few who seem fascinated and take every opportunity to stand quietly and watch every move of the builder/sewer.

It takes most of the month for everyone to complete his or her project. After the last nail is driven in and the last stitch knotted, I ask everyone not to take anything home until each has shown the class their finished product and talked about the difficulties and challenges of making something from scratch.

This turns out to be an interesting exercise, with a number of students simply saying, "Here is my apron/bird house. I liked making it." or "Making it was fun." Realizing I have not been specific enough and needed to suggest more pertinent questions if I want specific answers, I announce that, next Monday, I will be posting a series of questions on the board and that students who have made an item will be required to write a paragraph explaining how they worked through their project. These paragraphs will be read to the class a week from today. This garners groans and negative looks, so I add that in the meantime, the completed items will be on display: the bird houses on the window sills and the aprons on the card table and empty desk. This, of course, means that for one more week we'll be in our present chaos, but I feel it important for the students who participated to think through what they have done and accomplished.

The following week I notice, at recess and noon hour, repeated short sessions in which a younger student is quietly asking questions regarding a particular project. It makes me wish I had thought of this last year, however, I realize that for some students I have planted an idea, something new to think about and possibly to do in the future. This is one of the main goals of education, I think, and I'm pleased that I have been able to provide the opportunity, as basic as it has been.

The paragraphs turn out to be slightly better in length than the previous week's spoken statements. As each student comes to the front with a helper holding the apron or bird house, I see in some a shyness about describing their created item; others are nonchalant and matter-of-fact while a few boast a bravado regarding their accomplishment. Everyone seems pleased and several of the younger ones ask when it will be their turn. I say that, hopefully, in their new schools, there will be an opportunity.

Whenever I mention "new school" there are invariably looks of dismay, even annoyance. I always go on to say it will be a new adventure and that adventures are what make life interesting. I'm not sure it has much affect, but it does make me feel better. I know I would not be staying even if the school did remain open and so, in many ways, it's my adventure as much as theirs.

It's around this time that I have confirmed with my doctor that I am expecting our second child. This is still the era in teaching when a teacher should not be in a classroom once her pregnancy is showing. In another few months, my formerly slim waist will disappear and by May or June, I will definitely be "showing." In a graded school, I would discuss my situation with the principal, and a supply teacher would be called in. I *have* discussed this situation with my principal and decided I will carry on! Who is going to come and tell me to leave? The children, especially the older ones, will notice eventually, but I know no one is likely to say anything. I am in a perfect situation to break the rules and so I will.

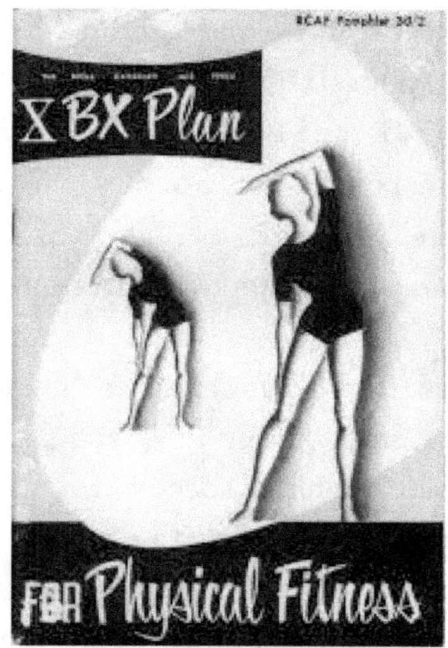

10BX fitness program

Physed in February

Once the home ec and shop projects are completed and relative order is restored, everyone wants to know when physed will start and what we will be doing. I begin giving this new project considerable thought. Because, whatever we decide to do will take an open space, we will, out of necessity, have to include all grades. Desks will have to be pushed out of the way, most likely toward the back on either side of the stove. Physical activity and a hot stove must be kept as far away from each other as possible. I will also need my desk pushed against the blackboard as it was positioned for the Beatles concert.

During the summer of 1962, in Morin Heights, Quebec, my husband, Jim, began using the military-based 5 BX exercise program. I had tried it but found it too male-oriented. Jim discovered and purchased 10 BX for me. I used it faithfully until I began teaching, and now, more than a year later, I locate it and decide these exercises will form the basis for my physed classes.

I bring both the 5 BX and 10 BX booklets to school and explain to the children that I will be using some of these exercises; that they were designed for men and women in the Royal Canadian Air Force and gives them a vigorous air of authority. Everyone, especially the boys, is keen to try it.

The 5 BX (Five Basic Exercises) plan was an exercise program was developed by Bill Orban in the late 1950s and first published in 1961. Orban was a Canadian athlete, scientist and academic who, after completing his studies in 1956, accepted a job offered by the RCAF. He took a position at the Department of National Defence and was tasked to develop a fitness programme for Royal Canadian Air Force pilots, a third of whom were deemed not physically fit to fly. His plan was developed first for men; subsequently, a corresponding program for women, under the name 10 BX (Ten Basic Exercises) was created.

Both programs were innovative in two respects. First, they did not require access to specialized equipment. Many RCAF pilots were located in remote bases in northern Canada with no access to gymnasium facilities, so it was important to offer a means of keeping fit without their use. Secondly, the exercise plan could be done in eleven minutes per day.

Twenty-three million copies of the booklets were sold to the Canadian public and it was popular around the world, being translated into thirteen languages. Orban, as a public servant, however, received no royalties from the success of these publications.

After reading both booklets, I decide to concentrate on the 10 BX plan that gives instructions for children beginning at age seven. The 5 BX gives a passing nod to those under twenty but is basically designed for adult males. I also decide that, even though the program is set up to be done for eleven minutes each day, we will do as much of it as is possible once a week on Wednesday afternoons, with a few of the exercises repeated on Mondays and Fridays.

Soon after the home ec and shop paraphernalia is gone, one of my senior students suggests that our exercise program should include somersaults. She says her cousin, who goes to one of the town schools where they have physed, says they do "forward rolls" on mats in the gymnasium. When I point out that we have neither a gymnasium nor mats, she suggests a mattress would work and that she knows where we can get one. I agree but don't anticipate this will happen. When I arrive at school the following Monday morning, however, a somewhat aging double bed mattress is leaning against our rarely used bookcase. Anticipating that the excitement of its presence will create the desire to punch and/or touch it, I print out a large sign, FOR PHYSED CLASS ONLY and pin it at the top of the mattress. I also move the desks closest to the mattress, more than an arm's length away—as temptation can be great.

Everyone, of course, already knows it's there, so its presence causes less excitement than I anticipate. It creates, however, an air of urgency regarding our start date. Having already more or less decided what we will do, I announce that the first formal physed class will be on Wednesday afternoon, after recess, and that the girls should wear or bring slacks to wear for this class. This causes excitement as well as a number of questions and comments.

"I thought we couldn't wear slacks to school."

"Can we come to school on Wednesday wearing our slacks?"

"Can we wear slacks other days as well?"

I have anticipated this as school rules in the 1950 and 1960's have always been strict regarding what females can and cannot wear. "On Wednesdays only," I say, "girls may wear slacks to school all day. I am your principal as well as your teacher, and I have decided this is the most practical dress for physed class day." I also explain that in high school, girls wear a gym outfit, a dreadfully ugly thing as I remember. I tell my students that I assume slacks are allowed in elementary school physical education classes.

The excitement builds first thing Wednesday morning when almost all the girls appear wearing slacks. As it is an exceptionally cold morning, most students remain inside once they arrive and there is a buzz among the girls comparing style, colour, and where the slacks were bought. Once everyone is inside, I notice that two junior girls are not wearing slacks. Just before morning recess, I tell each privately I'm sorry but they will have to forgo the forward roll part of physed. One says she forgot and the other says her mother hadn't done the washing yet. Both these children come from poorer families and I decide I will give each a reminder note to take home the following Monday.

Just before Wednesday afternoon recess, I ask the grade sevens and eights to stay in long enough to move desks and ready the room for this new class. As with other first time endeavours, anticipation creates an air of excitement. Good, I think, as the rest of the grades file out for recess, hopefully this excitement will translate into effort. Even though most of these children walk to and from school and play fairly vigorous games outside, I'm sure that these exercises will benefit them.

After recess, when everyone has draped and piled wet coats and snow pants on chair backs pulled as close to the stove as possible, I ask the children to sit in a circle in the now open space. As it's barely big enough to accommodate everyone, a number of younger siblings automatically move in front of an older sister or brother.

I stand in the middle of the group and explain that today we will do six exercises: the first four—toe touching, knee raising, side bends, and marching-on-the-spot—will be for everyone and the last two—half push ups and front rolls—for those who wish to try them. The rest may sit cross-legged on the floor and watch. I know that for a number of the younger students, coordination will be a problem and so I add that everyone is to try and do his or her best and, that if the exercise is too difficult, to stop and watch the others.

Because of the space constraint, I ask that the junior students make a circle in front of the seniors so that everyone has enough room. This takes time as a number of the younger ones have difficulty with the idea of being in a circle. I suggest they hold hands and move back a giant step. This works reasonably well.

We tackle toe touching first, ten repetitions, and I say they are to do what I do. When I raise my arms over my head, most follow while a few stretch their arms almost sideways, banging the person beside them. Remembering how difficult it was for many of the younger children to catch on to marching last year, I realize I must give specific instructions and show them exactly what to do. Even though I am standing with my arms straight up over my head, some children are obviously finding this difficult to follow. I stop and say, "Let's try that again and, this time, make sure the fingers of your hands are touching each other over your head." This has better results although a few still leave elbows bent, hands almost touching heads. "Stretch high," I urge them, "and bend slowly forward to touch the floor." Many of the older children have no problem and have completed the ten repetitions before I'm finished explaining the opening position. I stress that each repetition is to be done slowly, and that if older children complete their ten before the younger ones, they are free to do more.

Knee raises are next, and I emphasize and demonstrate that each knee should be raised so it is parallel to the floor. No one knows yet that I am pregnant, and I'm thankful these exercises are still easy for me. Knee raising is considerably more successful for the younger children than toe touching, and a number of them continue enthusiastically beyond the ten repetitions.

Side bends, requiring one to stretch an arm up and over one's head while simultaneously leaning to the same side, give many of the younger children problems. I realize that what is lacking in relation to their own bodies, is spatial perception. Even though I demonstrate the move several times, some lean forward, and few backward, with some bending sideways but to the wrong side. It's interesting how many permutations of a seemingly simple instruction are possible. Some of the older students snicker at these mistakes and a couple of the young ones sit and refuse to go on. I say firmly, "No snickering" and encourage the sitters to stand and carry on with the next exercise.

Marching on-the-spot works well with some students who quickly become bored with the on-the-spot aspect and begin turning in small marching circles. This catches on until almost everyone is twirling, with inevitable collisions and falls to the floor. I stop to restore order and point out firmly that twirling is not part of the exercise. I suggest that those bored by walking, jog on-the-spot, as it requires more endurance. We resume, and I notice that everyone is walking again after only a brief spurt at jogging. I can see that some, especially the younger ones, are now rapidly tiring. I ask everyone to sit in a cross-legged position.

Only a handful of older boys try the next exercise, half push ups. They all start with full push ups but, one by one, revert to the half position. Only Joe who is in grade eight and Keith who refuses to give in, manage the full ten.

I tell everyone to sit again in a large circle and I can see excitement building. The pièce de résistance is about to happen: forward rolls on an old mattress. I ask two of the senior boys to bring the mattress to the centre of the room, advising those close by to make room. The mattress, an aging Sealy, is somewhat depressed in the centre and has a long, brown stain across one corner. No one seems to mind and all lean forward to inspect our ensconced gym mat.

I vaguely remember doing forward rolls in high school gym class but do not feel, even though I do not yet look pregnant, that I want to demonstrate. When I ask for a volunteer, Marilyn and Nancy jump up. Marilyn steps forward and says she and her cousin were visiting relatives in October when the Summer Olympics were on somewhere, she says, but not in Canada. She explains that they watched some of the events on their aunt's TV and saw a young-looking girl gymnast doing forward rolls.

"And do you remember?" I ask.

Both girls nod vigorously and Marilyn gives her younger cousin a scornful look. "Are you sure you remember?"

"We played gymnastics at home afterward," Nancy says, narrowing her eyes and sticking out her chin. "I remember."

"All right," I say. "I think it would be fair to ask Nancy, who is younger to go first. Marilyn, once Nancy is off the mat, you may have your turn."

Nancy steps forward looking more than a little self-conscious. She stops at the edge of the mattress. "I need to take off my shoes," she says, and, slipping them off, steps onto the mattress. I watch her raise her arms over her head, crouch down, and tumble forward. She lands a little to one side but jumps up, raising her arms again and grinning. "Easy," she says, stepping off the mattress.

Marilyn follows with much the same result. As they both return to their places in the circle, several hands go up.

"Thank you Marilyn and Nancy, that was most helpful." I remember now doing forward rolls when I was in high school. I raise my arms straight over my head. "You begin like this," I say and then, crouching with my hands flat on the floor, continue. "You squat down like this and push forward so that your legs follow over your head. Our gym teacher always said it was important to keep your shoulders straight so that you land in a straight line." I stand up again, grinning. "No," I add, "I'm not going to demonstrate. Who wants to go next?"

A line forms, most of the older students and a few of the younger ones. Many do not, in any way, follow the instructions and end up coming sideways off the mattress or collapsing on their sides in their attempt. There are a few giggles but everyone is relatively polite.

When I suggest a second round, only five students line up. This exercise program has taken its toll. After the mat is dragged back into place and desks put into rows again, my weary bunch sits, many with their heads on their arms.

We end the day with me reading another chapter of our current novel.

Just before dismissal, I ask, "So, shall we have physed again next week?" Everyone says yes and I'm pleased that, in spite of the glitches, the lumpy mattress, and lack of coordination, my first physed class has been a success.

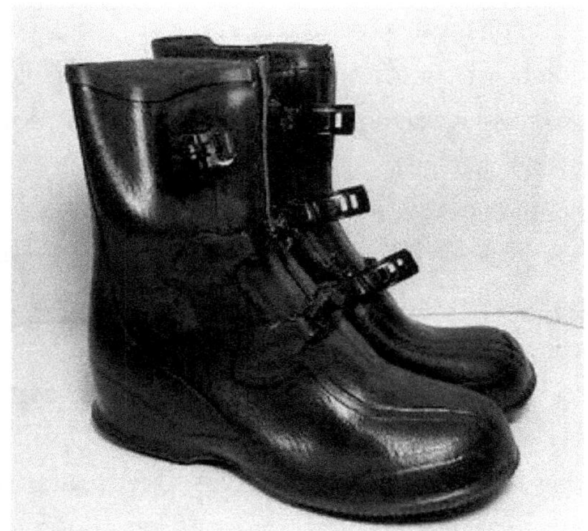

Galoshes

Muddy March—Psychology Course Panic

Spring comes early with rain melting the snow and rendering our playground a flat, low area, especially the baseball diamond, a muddy boot-pocked mess. For the children who don't own rubber boots, their shoes or galoshes are mud-caked, the metal fasteners on the latter, plugged and inoperable. After the first day of mud tracked everywhere in the room, our janitor, Mrs. Carr, leaves newspapers spread out in the hallway with signs "Muddy boots and shoes here," with arrows pointing to the floor. Most students co-operate, with those resisting being chastised and sent back by peers or siblings. The not-too-tidy row of boots leaves almost no room to walk and, on the first day, several juniors stumble and fall, resulting in tears, muddy clothes and boots scattered. Whenever someone goes to use the toilets, I warn him or her to be careful and not to trip.

At recess that morning, I send the children out grade by grade, with older siblings helping those who need it. This takes time, and recess ends up being over a half hour instead of fifteen minutes. Being principal of the school for almost a year and a half now, this doesn't bother me that much. I know time is mine to schedule as best I can.

Rain continues through the month with several snow and sleet days making things worse. Physed becomes a more regular activity, something to disperse pent up energy on days when everyone is inside from eight in the morning until dismissal at four.

Added to the dismal weather is the fact that my correspondence Psychology course has taken an unwelcome turn. Up until now, the assignments have seemed fairly easy. The subject matter is interesting and, the short essays I've been required to hand in, ten to date, have been marked by a teaching assistant who has consistently given me B+ and A-, noting that I am writing well. At this point in my life, I have no idea I will be a writer or that I have any talent for what I would consider such an esoteric career. The March segment is on statistics which I had not taken in high school. Math has always been my nemesis.

In grade-eleven, I passed Geometry by memorizing all the assignments we worked on in class, the teacher saying he would use these as a basis for the final exam. In grade-twelve, by this time sure I was completely incompetent in anything math-related, I barely passed Algebra. It was taught by a sympathetic teacher who told me quietly, after the final exam, that she was passing me so that I could continue into grade-thirteen. At this point, everyone including myself, expected I was headed for a stage career and so her generous spirit allowed me to go on to grade-thirteen where I took no math courses. It would be ten years before, as a mature student at university, I discovered it was dyslexia that gave me so much grief in high school spelling and math.

Being more focussed on my role as a teacher, I stumbled through the statistics assignments and rationalized that they would not be a major part of the final exam. The final exam was 150 multiple choice questions, one-third of which were based on statistics. To compound my misery I discovered, after the fact, that the ten assignments I had done so well in, counted for nothing and that the final exam was one hundred percent of my mark.

It was sometime in April, I received the news from Queen's that my mark was abysmally low, fifty-nine percent. I told no one and felt this confirmed I was not cut out for university. I decided that I would never put myself through this kind of humiliation again.

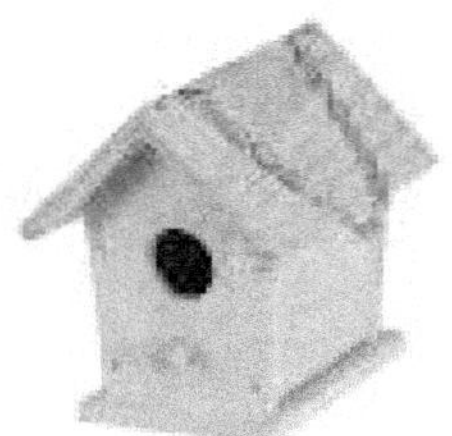

Bird House

April Projects

The second week of April, several of the older girls ask if I can bring the sewing machine back as they want to make aprons for their Moms for Mother's Day. This prompts the boys to request the tools again so they can make a gift as well. We move all the desks closer together again and, I am thankful that with warmer weather, the stove has died out by afternoon.

Because Mother's Day is the second Sunday in May, there is approximately a month for these projects to be completed. They will compete with Easter exams and day-to-day lessons, although most of the physed exercises can be done outside. The forward rolls have lost their initial appeal; once baseball and other outdoor games are resumed, no one requests them. Because of the space constraint of bringing back the sewing machine and wood-working tools, I quietly request that the student who brought the mattress, take it back. The next morning it is gone. No one makes a comment, although, given the verbal communication network in the neighbourhood, I'm sure everyone knows, and that likely some of the senior boys helped load it into someone's pickup truck after I left for the day.

The back corner next to the sink becomes the sewing area again with the opposite side near the bookcase for the bench, wood, and tools. Some afternoons, I find the noise level—sewing machine whirring, hammers banging and saws grating—difficult, but the children don't seem to mind, and we carry on.

When I come into my classroom each morning and look around, I wonder what an inspector would say about our creative clutter. I'm hoping no inspector does appear, as I know, especially if he is younger and on-the-way-up, he will not approve of my "condition." Too bad, I think, I'll be leaving anyway and won't be ever teaching in this jurisdiction again. It doesn't occur to me, as it does now, that this ruling regarding pregnant teachers was unfair to female teachers. Sexism is not part of 1960's vocabulary and Betty Friedman's, *The Feminine Mystique* published in 1963, is not something I have heard of, or am interested in.

The freedom I have in making executive decisions regarding teaching is unusual for the times, although many teachers of one-room schools before me undoubtedly have had more freedom than those in graded schools. Over and over, I have been required to make on-the-spot decisions with no one to consult regarding curriculum, activities and discipline, decisions that reflect not only on my teaching ability but also on my judgement. If I have pushed the limits either in protocol or expectations, no parent has complained; no board member has asked me to explain. Although my school is now passé in the Ontario educational system, I care fiercely for all my students and continue to give them the best education I can.

By now, most students have accepted the fact that their beloved one-room school is being closed. A few keep asking where they will be going and, as my board member, has no solid information, I give vague answers and tell everyone to concentrate on the present and not worry about the future.

In spite of the extra time taken to produce Mother's Day gifts, I notice that, increasingly, the senior students have finished their day's work well ahead of our four o'clock closing. During Easter holidays, when my son Bruce is at Mrs. Cable's daycare, I visit the town library to find information on Mother's Day. My thought is to create a project around the history of Mother's Day. Given the internet would have been considered science fiction at the time and having students use the local library not being an option, I decide to peruse the library in order to decide the best way to create this project.

The library, still in its original location on Cobourg's main drag, King Street, is cramped and heavy with too many books in too small a space. The new library, to be housed on Chapel Street in the former Trinity United Church Sunday school, is in its final phase of renovation and reconstruction. I've read several articles about its progress in the *Cobourg Sentinel Star*. Unfortunately, I will not visit this new location or see staff and volunteers wheel fourteen thousand books along the main street and up Division St. to Chapel St. by trolley and shopping cart on its moving date of July 22nd. Whether they waited for a sunny day or were lucky, I have no idea, as we had moved to Scarborough by that time. As was typical of the times, no pictures were taken of what must have been a rather spectacular event.

That day, I ask the librarian about the history of Mother's Day. She finds me a rather antiquated-looking book giving historical information, including the origins of the day, but nothing recent. She then suggests I try the children's section. Here I find an overly simplified book called *All About Mother's Day*. However, it does contain some more recent and interesting facts not covered in the first book. I take both out, knowing. I'll have two weeks to go through them before the five cent a week fine comes into effect.

After reading as much of the first book as seems relevant and going through the second, I decide that, in order to include everyone in this project, I will make up a list of Mother's Day questions for each family to take home; I will give a reasonable deadline for information to be collected and then compile answers on the black board. This done, I will add some of the interesting information that I have read in these books. I'll request that older students make short notes of the new information in their notebooks; this will be a good opportunity to introduce my senior students to "note taking" as a useful practice for studying and recording information. I'll request that a student from each family write up his or her information, and I'll pin up a display between the windows on the west side. Younger students can draw and colour a picture about Mother's Day from something that appeals to them in the information we have compiled, and I'll add this to the display.

Preparing this take-home form, of course, requires me to use the dreaded mimeograph machine—making a stencil and then working the rotating drum to get copies. I find the process both labourious and nerve-wracking, but as I am secretary as well as teacher and principal, I know I must do it. After school, I will begin.

I write out, in draft form, some basic questions regarding Mother's Day: when is it? How does your family celebrate? Why do you think it's important? I add to this list questions that are more speculative and more interesting: what can you or your family tell us about Mother's Day in your parents' time, your grandparents' time? Why did Mother's Day start in the first place?

This draft, printed out on a piece of lined paper, takes the best part of an hour. I want to make sure the information is clear and not too wordy. As well, I must contain everything I want to say to one stencil sheet. I have half a box of stencils left, and, with final exams coming up in June, I must be careful. There is no way at this time of the year that I would be able to request and get another box, especially as the school will be closed permanently.

As I must pick up my son Bruce at Mrs. Cable's by five, I take the draft with me and will read it to Rosamonde and Tante to get their opinions. They both tell me that because Mother's Day is on a Sunday, it has always been part of a church service, and that the minister usually preaches a sermon related to caring for others. During this service, mothers will be acknowledged but not given central priority. The custom is that if one's mother is alive, one pins a coloured flower to one's coat or jacket; if one's mother is not alive, a white flower. The flowers of choice are, traditionally, carnations.

After Bruce is in bed, I read aloud that in seventeenth century England, Mother's Day was reserved to honour the mother of Jesus Christ and that only later did it evolve to include all mothers. Tante, who is incredibly knowledgeable in all things religious, nods and says quietly that in those days it was celebrated on the fourth Sunday of Lent, the forty-day period prior to Easter. I wonder if she has read the book in my hands and comment on seeing this exact explanation in print. She smiles and urges me to continue. In North America, I read, it began in the 1800's, in the United States, when two women distressed by the death and suffering caused by the bloody Civil War, promoted "Mother's Friendship Day" in an effort to help reconcile both sides. It is interesting to read that one of these women, a Mrs. Howe, advocated for the concept of a "Mother's Day of Peace," which would be celebrated in early June. The article says it was largely intended as a way to get women united against war. Unfortunately, Mrs. Howe was never able to get Mother's Day of Peace made into a formal holiday. Her daughter lobbied the US government, and Mother's Day became official in 1914. It has become more and more commercialized in the following decades.

I ask Rosamonde how they celebrated Mother's Day when my husband and his two sisters were small, and she says that during the war years—that is, up until 1945—the children made cards at school, and she was not allowed to cook supper. As long as Rosemonde's mother was alive and living with them, the celebration was centred on grandmother Groulx. Later, when Mr. Manning was home from the war, the celebration became more elaborate, with the children helping him prepare supper.

The following day after school, I complete the stencil and make copies, the acrid smell of duplicating fluid filling the warm afternoon air.

As I have thirty students but only fifteen families this year, I make twenty copies in case someone loses or damages one.

On Friday, there are groans, of course, when I hand out the stenciled copies saying this is a special Mother's Day project and everyone, even the young ones, will be able to participate and help. I explain that, at home, one member of each family is to record answers to the given questions in a scribbler, and that I will make a chart on the side board compiling all the information. I purposely hand out this flyer shortly before dismissal, knowing it will elicit endless questions and comments which I don't want to deal with until the information is compiled. To insure that everyone understands the questions, I instruct that families group together around the room with the eldest quietly reading the questions to his or her siblings. This works fairly well, but, as soon as everyone is back in their seats, hands go up wanting to tell me things about their family's Mother's Day.

"Dismissal time," I say. "Save your comments until we have completed the project. I want everyone to bring this paper and your answers, written in a scribbler, back to school next Wednesday." The inevitable groans follow. "We will work on this for one or two afternoons and make our Mother's Day cards the first week in May. That gives you the weekend plus two days to complete this project. I'm sure your parents and grandparents, if they are nearby, will be happy to share their Mother's Day experiences with you." I ignore the noisy chatter as the children exit. This has definitely giving them something to think about.

On Wednesday, after afternoon recess, I ask everyone to clear their desks and for those who have sheets and answers to produce them. A little over half of the students have remembered to bring the sheets but almost all have made notes in their scribblers.

Everyone wants to tell me about getting Mother's Day gifts and what is done on this special day. Flowers and gifts are at the top of everyone's list: a bouquet of dandelions, flowers picked from the family garden, wildflowers gathered in the woods or from the roadside. The Met store, which sells a variety of inexpensive things, is mentioned again and again. Most children have been given, at the most, fifty cents to spend, and treasures include a large bottle of perfume, diamond earrings, slippers, and china figurines.

The second most important item is a Mother's Day card, and everyone tells me they always make these at school as well as help younger siblings make one at home. Red construction paper seems to be most popular, and I make a note to remember this when we are making cards at the beginning of May.

As well as gifts, many children prepare "breakfast in bed" for their mother, pancakes being the preferred choice. Those who cook breakfast emphasize that they also do the cleanup. Several tell me that this is the best part for their mother and many pitch in to help their Dad cook as only a few families can afford to go out for supper. One or two say their Mother prepares supper the day before, and all they have to do is heat it up, serve it and, of course, do the cleanup.

Those who go to church also mention getting a coloured flower from the garden to wear in honour of their mother. Some of their Moms and Dads wear white flowers, but, for many, it is only grandparents who do. I am not aware this is a community with young parents and relatively young grandparents. Of course, in the sixties, anyone forty or older is considered old. As well, dress codes dictate that certain ages wear certain clothes. No one wears jeans except farmers in the barn. Daring women wear slacks. As I have already mentioned, girls and female teachers in schools are required to wear skirts or dresses.

The blackboard chart is quickly filled. Everyone wants to tell me his or her personal anecdote about Mother's Day. I have a difficult time getting them to stop at four, and I promise we will continue tomorrow.

The second afternoon is given exclusively to personal anecdotes from the children. Again, I ask everyone to sit in groups according to families; one person from each family will tell the stories. This works reasonably well, although, often, a younger family member will break in with their particular version of what happened.

For the last half hour, I tell them how and why Mother's Day began in the first place. I read several passages from one of the library books, telling of the women who struggled to have Mother's Day made a special day. Some are surprised that there hasn't always been a Mother's Day. "It has been around for a very long time," I say, "even back to your great-grandparents time." This elicits a discussion about old people and life a hundred years ago. There is so much more I could do to teach these children. They are interested and questioning, which is always the beginning of real learning. I must, however, follow the curriculum; teach the required subjects; set exams and hand the report cards over to my board member who will distribute them along with the Ontario Student Record (OSR) cards to the schools my children will be attending in the fall. I suggest that anyone who is interested in family history could begin a personal project, that of finding out about their own family history and writing it down. Several nod, but I will have no idea whether or not anyone follows through.

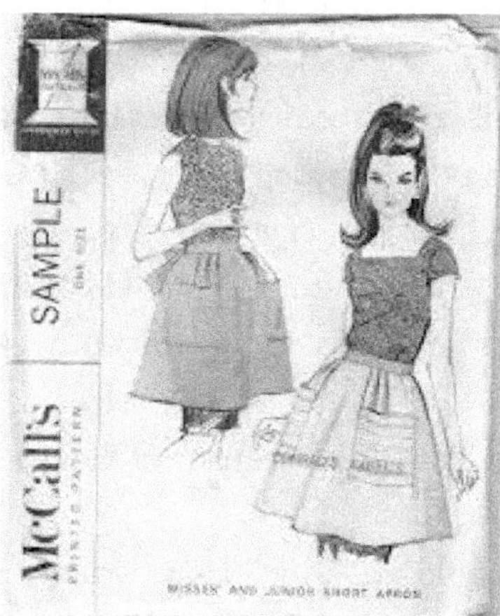

Apron pattern

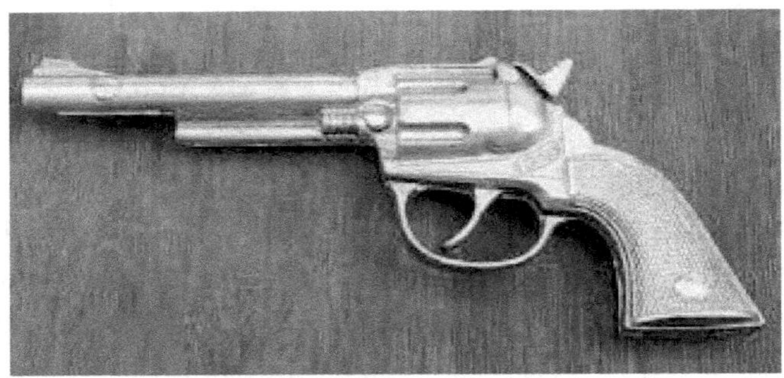

Picture of cap gun

Cowboys, Cap Guns and Mice

Once April and the warmer weather arrives, everyone is outside playing baseball, skipping, playing hopscotch, tag, and a game I had no idea about. The boys are wound up, and, most days, the noise coming through the open window reaches a fever pitch. I know now that it is just a home run or that someone has unexpectedly ground out and no longer rush to the window to see if a disaster has occurred.

One April afternoon, following recess, everyone is busy at work; the room is quiet except for the scratching of pencils and the occasional scraping of a chair. Without warning, a loud gunshot-like bang breaks the silence. I'm sure it's from inside our classroom. I jump up knocking a pile of scribblers to the floor. A couple of grade-ones emit shrieks; almost everyone is wide-eyed while many of the older boys appear to be trying not to smirk.

"What in the world was that?" I say, walking rapidly down a side aisle. "Where did that noise come from?"

The room is momentarily silent until one of the juniors says, "Smoke, Mrs. Manning. Look, there's smoke."

I turn quickly to see Wayne staring fixedly at his desk while a delicate plume of smoke rises from his ink well. "Wayne," I say, approaching him. "Is there something in your desk that set off that dreadful noise?"

"Yes, Mrs. Manning."

"Well, hand it over," I say, now standing over him. "You've startled all of us. What is it?"

Wayne slowly puts his hand into his desk and pulls out...a gun.

"Good grief," I say, taking it. "It certainly looks authentic."

"It's just a cap gun, Mrs. Manning," Wayne says, trying to look nonchalant, "It can't hurt anyone."

"And how is it that it went off in your desk?"

"I don't know," Wayne says, still staring at his desk.

"Could it be you reached in and pulled the trigger?"

"On no, Mrs. Manning. I didn't touch it. I know I didn't."

"So it went off by itself? I find that hard to believe."

"I don't know how it happened." Wayne's voice is beginning to falter.

"A cap gun emits sparks. You could have started a fire."

He looks up at me with such a look of innocence. "I don't know how it happened, honest I don't."

"Well, you won't be doing anything with this gun for a while," I say, marching back to my desk. "It's confiscated until Friday dismissal, at which time you will take it home."

"Yes, Mrs. Manning."

"Are there any other cap guns in the school?"

"No, Mrs. Manning," several boys respond.

"Well, there better not be. If I see another cap gun in here or in the yard, the owner will not only lose it permanently, he...or she... will have no recess or noon hour for the next month."

I noisily pick up the strewn scribblers. "And Wayne?" I slap the pile onto my desk.

"Yes, Mrs. Manning?"

"You will stay after school, and we will have a talk."

"Yes, Mrs. Manning."

The room remains totally quiet for the remaining hour. When I announce dismissal, everyone slips out, a few whisper, that's all. Wayne remains at his desk, looking more than a little uncomfortable. I've never had occasion to discipline Wayne before. He's a typical eleven-year old, full of energy, given perhaps to the odd prank, but nothing like this. It seems, to me, out-of-character.

I wait until everyone is outside and pull an adjacent desk chair over to sit beside him. "Wayne, the cap gun couldn't have gone off by itself."

He stares at his desk, his elbows and fists pressing against its scarred surface.

"Did someone put you up to this?"

He shakes his head.

"If they did, I'm aware you're not going to tell."

"I'm sorry. It won't happen again."

"No cap guns in the school."

"Never."

"And no outdoor recess or noon hour for you until the end of the week."

"Will you make me write lines?" he asks, looking repentant and relieved.

"I'll find useful things for you to do. I think some of the windows could use a wash."

He looks at the six large windows, three on either side and nods, catching his breath.

"You're dismissed," I say, standing and pushing the chair back to where it belongs.

He nods and bolts for the door.

I sit at my desk wondering what, if anything, I should do about this. Obviously, there are a number of cap guns stashed in the yard and they are used at recess and noon hour. It's impossible for me to see the entire playground from inside. Even when I look out the west window, I can't see all the way to the school property line. There's a rise in the land, and it's there, safely out of sight against the west fence, that the forts were built last year and likely reinforced this year. It's most likely that's where they go to play cowboys, firing cap guns at each other in mock ferocity, someone yelling, "You're dead," with the victim falling momentarily to the ground. I remember playing these games when I was a kid. No supervision, no one to tell us it was wrong.

I know I must not make rules I can't enforce, and banning cap guns outside is one of those. I sigh and gather up my things including the cap gun which I stuff into my purse. I'll leave it in the car until Friday, in the trunk under the mat. But what if I'm stopped and my car is searched? Highly unlikely. Instead, I take the gun to the back cupboard and shove it under the box that holds Christmas decorations.

"Another day," I say to myself, locking the door. "What else could possibly happen?"

As it turns out, two days later, I'm in for an even bigger surprise. Mrs. Carr has warned me, on several occasions, that there are mice getting into the school. I have seen no evidence of this but have warned everyone not to leave any lunch remnants in their desks or on the shelf over the coat hooks.

In the middle of the afternoon, when everyone is quietly working, a loud stomp on the floor brings me to my feet to see what is going on this time. Keith Wilson's foot is planted firmly in the aisle, and several girls in the vicinity are exclaiming and turning their heads away.

"Got him," Keith says triumphantly, grinning at me. "One less mouse is this school."

I approach him. "You've stomped on a mouse?"

"You bet," Keith says. "Wanna see it?" He bends down and moves his foot. A decidedly dead mouse lies flattened on the floor, parts of it exuding from its flattened grey fur.

I take a deep breath and look around. Most students are working furiously, obviously trying to ignore this grizzly act. A couple of the little ones are close to tears.

"Take it outside," I say firmly. "Right now."

Keith grins and picks up the dead mouse by its tail. "I know you don't approve," he says, walking rapidly toward the door, "but Mrs. Carr sets traps, and the Carr boys empty them each morning." He stops at the doorway. "We don't want mice running around in the school, do we?" And he's gone momentarily. "I chucked him down the can," he says returning, still looking pleased with himself.

"Get some paper towels and wipe the floor," I say. "Then wash your hands." I return to my desk but remain standing, wondering what I should or could say. What Keith says is true but it never has occurred to me that someone would kill a mouse during class. Part of me is impressed by his fast twitch muscles, fast enough to down a moving mouse. I'm quite horrified, however, by this overt act of violence, no matter how insignificant it is to Keith and possibly to a number of my students. Farm life doles out life and death on a regular basis. I know this but it still somewhat offends me. I decide the best way to deal with it is to ban the practice and hope no more mice appear.

Once Keith has wiped the floor, washed his hands and returned to his seat, I make my proclamation. "I know it is important for this classroom to be free of mice, but from now on I ban stomping on a mouse in this classroom." In spite of the obvious ridiculousness of this statement, the room is completely quiet, everyone waiting to see what I will say to Keith. He has folded his hands demurely on his desk and doesn't look at all worried. Because of this, I consider handing him some punishment. After a few moments of deliberate silence, I continue. "I won't punish you this time, Keith," I say, "but if you or anyone else in this room tries or succeeds in stomping a mouse to death, you will regret it."

Keith nods respectfully in my direction and pulls out his reader, opening it and looking as though he is fully absorbed. I sit down and attempt to resume whatever it was I was doing five minutes ago. Everyone else settles down to work again. I wonder if he will be considered a hero, lauded, and slapped on the back after school. I'm sure no one will breathe a word of this to their parents. By tomorrow, I will have forgotten and I'm sure Mrs. Carr will have removed the small irregular blood stain on the floor close to his desk. Life in a country school is not for the faint-hearted.

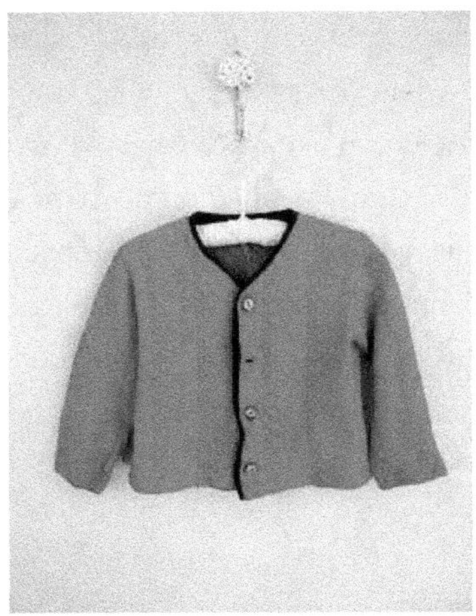

The red sweater

The Red Sweater

May, as well as being a push to complete all subjects in all grades, brings the usual round of outdoor activities: hopscotch on the cement pad at the front, ball toss against the west school wall, and baseball.

Near the end of May, at recess on a hot afternoon, Debbie, one of my grade-three girls, runs in with an excruciating look on her usually sunny face.

"Mrs. Manning," she says, fighting back tears, "I've dropped my sweater down the toilet."

The toilets, at this time of year, are considerably less than pleasant and, whenever I have to use one, I try to hold my breath for the entire time I'm there. Accumulation and warm weather have heightened their nearly-full outhouse stench.

Being hungry most of the time now, I'm enjoying a second sandwich for lunch. I put the rest of it back in my lunch pail. "Are you sure?" I ask. "Maybe you left it outside." This is a ridiculous thing to say, really, a highly unlikely dodge.

At this point, Debbie bursts into tears. "It's my red sweater," she sobs. "My new one from Christmas, and Mommy will be so mad. I'll get a licking, I know I will."

"Can you see it?" I ask, standing and trying not to feel queasy. I was eating a salmon sandwich and can still smell fish on my fingers.

"I…I think so," she continues, hiccupping between sobs. "Can you get it for me Mrs. Manning, can you?"

"All right," I say, retrieving a flashlight from one of my desk drawers. "Let's go and have a look."

The lid is up and the smell is overpowering. The windows are never opened here in the warm season as the place would be overrun with flies. As it is, there still are a few, whacking themselves against the glass trying to get out. I bend over, holding the flashlight in one hand, my other steadying my less than agile stance, and peer into the hole. My expanding belly is definitely in the way. Along with the brown and blackish excrement and the crumpled folds of yellowed toilet paper, I glimpse something woven and red.

"I think I can see it," I say, standing upright again. I take a gulp of the putrid air and feel slightly nauseous.

Debbie grabs hold of me, wrapping her thin arms around my hips. "You can get it for me, can't you Mrs. Manning? I know you can." She lets go and sobs more pitifully.

"A coat hanger," I say more to myself than to my distraught student. "I might be able to reach it with a coat hanger."

Behind my desk on a big coat hook there are empty coat hangers. I push past the distraught Debbie and retrieve one of them, undoing it and un-bending the curves so that I have a long straight piece with a hook at one end.

Flashlight in one hand and retrieval hook in the other, I return to the smelly scene of the crime to bend over, sufficiently, so that my face is almost level with the toilet seat, leaving just enough room for my flashlight hand in one side and my retrieval hook in the other. The first couple of attempts are unsuccessful, with the hook slipping past the sweater and miring itself in brown sludge. I stand, again, needing air, and for some kind of resolve that is very close to eluding me.

"It is there, isn't it?" Debbie says, tears stopping momentarily. "You can see it, can't you?" She grabs hold of me again and sobs into my skirt.

"Yes," I say, "and I think I can get it this time." I bend down again, bracing myself for the upsurge of that distinctively foul smell. This time, once the hook is against the sweater, I twist the coat hook and slowly, ever so slowly begin pulling it toward the surface. Just as it's nearly up to the surface, the wretched thing slips off the hanger and disappears into the mire.

Have you got it? Debbie asks. Her little fists are clenched; her mouth in a tight line.

"I had it," I falter, "but it slipped off the hanger and…" I peer into the depths again. "I can't even see it now."

"So, it's gone?" she says, tears welling again. "My red sweater is gone?"

At this point, her older brother, Wayne, appears, presumably looking for his sister. The washroom door is open and he can see us standing there.

"Sorry," he says, turning abruptly.

"It's okay, Wayne," I say. "Your sister dropped her sweater down there, and I was trying to get it out."

"Her sweater?" Wayne says, making a face. "You wouldn't want it after it's gone down there." He backs away from the open door.

"Mommy'll be so mad," Debbie says, tears running down her face. "It was my good red sweater."

"You coming out now?" he says. "We're playing tag."

"I don't want to play tag," Debbie says, She's crying harder now. "I-I don't want to do anything." She runs into the classroom and, throwing herself into her seat, sobs and hiccups with greater intensity.

"You go out, Wayne," I say, "I'll look after Debbie."

Wayne shrugs and runs back outside.

"Debbie," I squat beside her desk. "Debbie, I will write a note to your mother explaining what happened. It wasn't your fault. It was an accident, and accidents happen."

She sits up and stops crying. "Maybe Mrs. Carr can get it out when she comes later. Could you ask her? Could you?" Her face is dirt-streaked, the lids of her large blue eyes are red and inflamed.

"I will ask her," I say, handing her some Kleenex. "Why don't we go to the sink and wash your face with cold water."

She takes my hand and glues her small body to mine as we walk to the sink.

When everyone is back in for the afternoon, I quietly tell Debbie I will have the note ready for her to take home after school. She nods and looks away, and I know there is nothing I can do to help her deal with this. It's one of those harsh lessons all children have to learn, that some things go wrong and can never be fixed, not by them or by an adult. It's hard to come to terms with, even for adults, and for children, the first few times it happens can be devastating. During the afternoon, I stop by her desk a number of times and, once or twice, feel her small hand momentarily clutch my skirt.

Several times before dismissal, she asks to go to the washroom and I'm sure she's still looking, still peering down into the putrid depths. I write the note and put it in a sealed envelope for her to take home. She comes up to my desk and smiles as I hand it to her, then turns resolutely and marches out behind the others.

No one has said anything about the incident, even though it's likely that someone heard her crying and asked her brother about it. Whether, as my senior girls repeatedly say, *it's just too gross to talk about* or whether no one has noticed. I'm sure it's one incident I will always remember and probably, at some later point, laugh about. Now, I'm just relieved and feel, this afternoon, very pregnant.

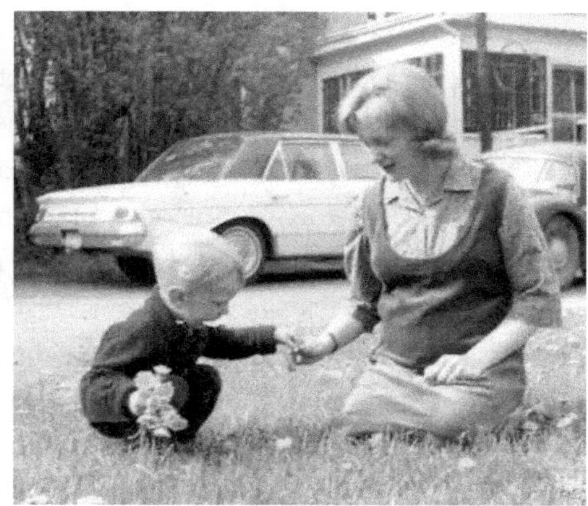

Bruce and pregnant momma

The Inspector's June Visit

By June, I am feeling considerably less agile and sit more than I stand. The fact that this is the last month for me and my students in this school has little impact on the day-to-day routine, however. I fill the black boards with seat work before nine each morning, and the marking of notebooks, even with my trusty helpers, continues to be monumental.

At the beginning of the month, using last year's exam questions as a guide, and keenly aware that I tend to make questions too difficult or too complicated, I begin the labourious task of setting up exams, one page of questions for each subject, carefully printed in my exam notebook to then be copied onto stencils. I print rather than write which would be faster because, in so doing, I can more accurately gauge the number of letters on each line in the stencil. The stencils are legal paper size rather than the standard 8 1/2 by 11 so, in order to make accurate lines on each stencil sheet, I tape two lined notebook pages together and cut them to the size of the stencil sheet. Next, I fold the taped result in half and place it partially over the stencil, so that I can mark dots on the left and right-hand sides to the bottom of each page. When I connect the dots from left to right, I have lined stencils. Needless to say, this preparation, plus copying the printed lines onto each stencil, takes time and patience, repetitious work for which I don't have much tolerance. However, by completing one exam each evening after Bruce is asleep, I manage to finish the sixteen individual exam pages by the middle of the month.

The second week of June, after recess in the afternoon, there's a loud knock on the door and an officious-looking man wearing a stylish suit walks briskly past the toilet doors and into the back of the classroom. I know from his stance that he is the inspector.

"Mr. Bridgeport," he says loudly in a rather nasal voice. "Your inspector."

I stop teaching and ask the children to stand and say good afternoon to Mr. Bridgeport.

After a shuffle of chairs and shoes, everyone turns to our visitor. "Good afternoon, Mr. Bridgeport," they say, mostly in unison.

"Carry on," he says without smiling or acknowledging their greeting. "I'm here to observe."

Everyone sits, and I continue going over the afternoon's work, a grade eight geography lesson concerning Canadian mountain ranges. I have a chart on the board:

Mountain Range: Name: Location: Characteristics: Interesting Details:

We have just listed the three main groups: the Rockies, the Laurentians and the Yukon St. Elias range. My five grade sevens and eights, who have this chart copied in their notebooks, are looking through pages of our ancient encyclopaedias for the location of each. As each is found, we have a discussion about the location and whether anyone in their family or extended family has visited or lives in any of these locations. This has provoked quite a lively discussion with several of the younger children, wildly waving their hands to comment as well. I suggest that if anyone has a more recent encyclopaedia, and is allowed to bring it to school, we would all benefit from more details. Several children say they have photographs in a family album; one can bring a *National Geographic* article while another thinks there are some postcards from a distant relative. I suggest we will make a table display of this material. Wolfgang, who has been avidly listening, asks if he can make a chart showing the relative heights of the three mountains. I mention to the Inspector that Wolfgang is our resident artist and that we always welcome his contributions. The Inspector who, to this point, has remained stone-faced, giving the impression he is here but not particularly interested in anything we are doing, nods and asks why Wolfgang is not part of the group. I tell him that Wolfgang is in grade-six and that this is a grade-seven/eight lesson. I add that often when Wolfgang has finished his day's work, he listens to lessons of older classmates. The Inspector nods and makes notes in a book he is carrying. I have no idea whether Wolfgang's participation is a positive or negative aspect of my teaching technique, and, at this point, I don't care.

Once school is dismissed and my black board monitors have been discreetly ushered out, I return to my desk to wait for whatever comments the Inspector will make. He, in turn, stays sitting cramped into an empty back desk, his knees jutting out on either side, scribbling more notes. I begin marking grade-four arithmetic scribblers, and, am so immersed, I don't hear him approach. He clears his throat, and I look up. "Would you like a chair?" I ask, trying to create a more relaxed atmosphere. "There's an extra one I can get."

"No need," he says and, standing in front of my desk, begins flipping through his pages. I know from the Psychology course I took at Queen's that by standing he maintains a superior stance over me. "I must say before I start," he begins, "that I am rather surprised by your current condition." He stares down at me. "You aren't going to have that baby on the desk, are you?"

I slap the notebook closed and stare at him for several seconds before answering. "As my due date is August twentieth and this is June ninth, I think it highly unlikely."

His body posture deflates momentarily before returning to its former dominant stance. "I see," he says, scribbling in his notebook. He looks around the room. "A bit cluttered, I must say, but I suppose it's the best you can do."

"We do very well here, and I'm proud of my students. They all work hard."

"I see," he says. He walks to the black board as if to more closely inspect my chart. "You do know this school is to be closed?" he says as if he's sure I'm not privy to this information.

"My board contact, Mr. Moore, informed me of this at the beginning of May." His arrogance is beginning to wear me down.

"I see," he repeats, and I wonder, fleetingly, if he has only this one response.

"Would you," I ask, "have any idea where my students will be placed?"

He slaps shut his book. "That information is not in my jurisdiction," he says. He stares down at me again. "Thank you. That will be all." He turns and marches toward the exit.

"Thanks for visiting our school," I call out, "and have a good summer holiday."

He closes the door without replying.

Once he is gone, I sit at my desk, hands shaking, expletives running though my head. "Are you going to have that baby on your desk?" I say aloud. There is no answer to this type of ridiculous hyperbole. I'm angry and humiliated but, at the same time, wonder if he will black-list me so that I won't be able to teach again. Even though I have never thought about feminism, or that being female gives me the right to stand up against an arrogant male in authority, there is a part of me that is furious, that wants to strike out at this indignity, this abuse of power. Instead, I carefully stack the arithmetic books to take home for marking, make sure the windows are all closed, gather up my lunch pail, and lock the door of my dear little school.

"Inspector be damned," I mutter under my breath as I get into our car that, up until a few weeks ago, my husband Jim was driving. I have, suddenly, become too front heavy to double myself enough and get into our hardtop MG, and so we have switched vehicles. Today this seems like yet another indignity I must endure. I slam the door harder than necessary. I need to calm down before I pick up my son. He has incredible radar sensors and will know, immediately, if I am upset. On the drive into town, I concentrate on the June lushness of everything, the blue sky, even the overly-warm afternoon.

When I pull up at Mrs. Cables,' a number of children are playing inside the open back yard, Mrs. Cable close by. As soon as Bruce sees our car, he dashes to the edge where the lawn meets the back lane. Mrs. Cable is there in a flash, bending over him, probably telling him to wait until I come into the yard. His excitement and enthusiasm diffuse the last of my irritation. As we head home, his ongoing chatter outlining his day, thankfully reactivates my perspective as a mother. The inspector and his terse words fade, and I am immersed in hearing his version of "good stuff" and "nut butter cookies" and "me riding the trike." By the time we pull into the Manning driveway, I've forgotten all about the inspector and remind myself to ask Rosamonde and Tante what they know about the Rockies and Laurentians.

Our Final Days

June 30th, the last day of school, falls on a Wednesday this year, and so exams will be the week before. This will give me five days to mark and fill in report card results. During exams, I will give letter grades to the subjects that have no exams.

Mr. Thrip has been less demanding with his expectations and he must be relieved this will be his last year dealing with one-room schools. He does, however, look at my now visible belly with some disapproval. I'm sure he thinks I should not be teaching in my condition but is prudent enough to say nothing. Besides, I have given music enough priority during the year that my students have performed exceptionally well, both in singing and theory. Next year, these students will be moving to schools where he will be teaching. This technical improvement has to be a plus from his point of view. I know these technical skills are necessary and hope my students will carry the pure joy of singing with them to their next school, wherever that may be.

No one asks any more to what school they will be transferred. They know they will likely be split up, sisters and brothers, depending on the grade, separated and sent to different schools. Being children, they have accepted the inevitable. What choice do they have? I won't likely teach again for a number of years, except perhaps as a supply teacher depending on where we are living. Basically, we all ignore it. This one-room school has been the centre of learning to most of these children for years longer than I've been here, and, after less than two years, I already feel it's the best place to be. However, although fate and bureaucratic decision-making have interfered, my students have their lives ahead of them, and this, in part, will soften the blow of leaving this familiar place.

The week following the Inspector's visit, I am again seriously wondering what we can do to celebrate the end of this school year. We will have three school days left the week following exams. If I give out report cards on the last day, then the day before would be the best day for a school outing.

Friday afternoon, before our weekly baseball game, I ask the class for suggestions for an end-of-the-year outing. I emphasize it must be something we can do easily within the Cobourg/Port Hope area. A fishing trip is suggested, also a hike somewhere, and then someone says, "What about a picnic at Victoria Park in Cobourg?" I thank everyone and, during the game, think seriously about the benefits of the picnic suggestion. It would include all grades; parents, mostly mothers of course, could provide transportation and lunch; the park has tables, washrooms, playground equipment, a grassy area for games, and the beach.

Lake Ontario will still be brutally cold, and I will have to emphasize no wading in the water as tempting as that will be, especially if the day is hot. Wading invariably leads to pretending to fall in, and, if one student does so, there will be the inevitable string of copycats. Beach walking will have to be well chaperoned. However, given that the June water temperature in Lake Ontario, even at this sandy beach, is usually no more than fifty or fifty-five degrees Fahrenheit, it is unlikely that after a few finger samplings anyone will want to venture in. If we leave the school at 11 a.m. after morning recess, we'll be set up at our picnic tables by noon. After lunch we can play games. I decide I will formally announce the picnic and ask the children what games they would like to play.

On Monday, following afternoon recess, I say that, on Tuesday June twenty-ninth, providing we can find enough parents who can drive, we will have a picnic and games at Victoria Park in Cobourg. The response is overwhelmingly positive with three or four students assuring me that their mothers will be one of the drivers. With five children to a car, there being, of course, no seat belts, we can manage with six cars, mine being one of them.

Because I know that who goes in which car could pose a problem, I say that I need to know by Friday morning which mothers will be driving. I will put the car names, including mine, on the black board, along with names of children in each given family car. For the remaining students, we will draw car positions from a box. This will, I hope, eliminate favouritism and eliminate some students being not picked.

When I ask for suggestions for games to play, a three-legged race, an egg and spoon race and a sack race are the three mentioned most often. There is extended discussion as to whether we should use raw or boiled eggs. Raw eggs, of course up the ante considerably, but they also set up the prospect of slipping on a broken egg or having one splat down a blouse or shirt. After arguments pro and con are voiced, I ask for a vote, and cooked eggs win by a narrow margin. I notice that the boys overwhelmingly voted for raw eggs while the girls opted for cooked. I also know, but don`t point out, that there are more girls than boys in this group. I can see some of the boys are quite disgruntled, but we move on to the next item and they refrain from saying more. A couple of girls mention a hula hoop contest and I say if someone brings a hula hoop we can see who is interested. Sacks for the sack race are no problem as a number of farm kids can bring feed sacks. I ask those interested in the three-legged race whether they should bring a long scarf of soft material for tying legs together. The boys want to use rope, and I say that`s fine as long as they`re wearing long pants. We don`t want to be dealing with rope burns on bare legs.

Essie Stoaker has been absent this school year, even more than she was last; Gerald, as expected, did not return in the fall. Essie has not been in school regularly since January and not at all since the middle of May. I assume, therefore, that she will be absent. I have been less stressed about her this year as I realize there is nothing I can do. In the fall, when I mentioned her to the school nurse, she rolled her eyes and said only "that bunch." I realize this does not begin to address the obvious problem this family faces, but, given my work load and personal responsibilities, even when my conscience says I should be doing something, I ignore the problem and carry on. The few times Essie does show up, I encourage her as best I can but she is so far behind and not much interested in learning. If I ask her anything about home or is there anything I can do, she hangs her head and says nothing.

Exam week comes sooner than I want it to, but as we have been reviewing for most of the month, the results are reasonably good. I spend the entire last weekend in June marking and entering marks on report cards. Jim is home from his new job in Toronto and, thankfully, takes Bruce to the beach and for drives. It's impossible to explain to a not-yet-three year-old why I can't join them. Distraction is the best method, and Jim has become good at it, suggesting an outing whenever Bruce begins to demand my attention. The "mother" part of me will be relieved when school is over and I can resume full-time parenting responsibilities. We have begun looking for a house to buy in Toronto and have narrowed it down to several sprawling subdivisions in Scarborough, east of the city, partly because the prices are reasonable and partly to be closer to Cobourg and family visits.

Monday of the last school week, before we do a yard cleanup in the morning, I ask for the Victoria Park picnic drivers' names and list them on the side board. Beneath, I add the names of students with each family and say that I will put the drivers' names in a box and that all other students will draw which car they will be in. There is a bit of grumbling, with some students wanting to drive with friends, and I distract everyone with a list of outside yard cleaning jobs.

Indoor cleanup in the afternoon involves individual student desk cleanup, followed by sorting through too many items that have been stuck in various cupboards and on shelves over the past two years. There is a pile of unclaimed things: sweaters, shoes, hair clips, mitts, bowls and spoons from soup days, artwork and scribblers with no name, even a baseball glove. Most are retrieved and I have students help me load my car with the belongings I have brought to the school over the past two years: the kettle, soup pot and ladle, several large piles of books, mainly children's books for the library, the record player and records, and, up on a shelf, the ukulele used for the Beatles concert. Irene takes it and strums its badly out-of-tune strings. There's a sudden hush as we are caught in this moment of endings, an inevitable nostalgia for the irretrievable. She smacks its back and runs, laughing, outside to put it into my car.

Before dismissal, I remind everyone that, tomorrow, they are to bring a lunch and a drink. The girls are to wear shorts or slacks; those who said they could are to bring sacks for the race and a hula hoop. I will provide spoons and boiled eggs, as well as some extra scarves for the three-legged race.

At this point, it`s impossible to realize fully that in two more days my life here and the life of this school will end permanently. I gather up my lunch pail and hurry to my car, thinking only of picking up Bruce and organizing items for tomorrow, the same things I have been doing every weekday for the past two school years.

When I arrive the following morning, the excitement in the school yard is almost as high as it was for our Thousand Islands trip last year. A number of these children have likely never been to Victoria Park, especially the younger ones. There were a couple of parent notes, scribbled with poor spelling on used envelopes, voicing concern that Victoria Park and the beach are potentially dangerous places where one could fall into the water and drown or be attacked by some weirdo lurking in the shadows. I have to remember that the park and beach, which to me has always been a perfect place for picnics and swimming, could seem foreign and intimidating to someone whose perspective goes no further than shopping once a month in Cobourg or Port Hope. I have chosen to ignore these notes. As I see that the children of these concerned parents are here today, it confirms that this concern was something they had to get off their chests but had no real intention of acting upon.

Including my car, we have a luxurious six vehicle convoy, which means four and five children to each. Since a couple of the parents have roomy station wagons, we have been able to pick names so that everyone is comfortably accommodated.

Luck is with us and June 29th 1965 is a perfect day, sunny with a light breeze, capricious little waves lapping at the sandy beach shore. Once our picnic spot is found, and a few tables pulled together, I invite everyone to lay out their lunch and remove shoes and socks. When I announce that we will go down to the water for temperature testing, a few of the young ones shake their heads vehemently and stay close to the picnic mothers. When one mother asks me if this is a safe thing to do, given there are no lifeguards, I say I've already tested the water before

I came to school and it's only forty-five degrees. The result is as I expected. A number of the older boys rush down and wade in, backing out immediately, shaking their heads, yelling "Freezing!" The rest approach tentatively, a number of them bending over to run fingers through the clear, lapping waves. There is much chattering about ice cold water, several eulogizing the superiority of Rice Lake for being much warmer. This popular fishing lake is a forty-five minute drive north of Cobourg, and several families have cottages there. I only tried to swim in this lake once and found the long, slimy rice leaves close to the surface definitely not to my liking.

"All right," I say once everyone has backed away from the water, some still grimacing as though it was the enemy, "I think it's not going to be a wading day." I turn and walk up the beach with a crowd of noisy children pushing past me, now satisfied the water is too cold. Mothers are smiling and nodding when we return.

Our picnic lunch progresses reasonably well with only a few of the younger children spilling a drink or dropping a sandwich or cookie on the grass. I have brought two jugs of Freshie for after the games and dole some of it out when someone breaks into tears over a lost drink. Older siblings help out, and, within fifteen to twenty minutes, crumpled waxed paper and empty paper bags are taken ceremoniously to the large black garbage can and deposited. One of the mothers has brought an oversized cardboard box for her family's and car mates' lunches and offers to store any lunch pails or empty thermoses until we leave.

I ask a couple of the senior boys to retrieve two shopping bags from my car. With an industrial measuring tape from our home tool box, we measure the distance for the sack race. In the Manning garage, I found an old croquet set and have brought the upright stakes to use as markers for the beginning and end of our races. We mark the full distance, and a second set about halfway back for the younger children who will go first.

I have everyone sit cross-legged in a circle inside the racing area. Blowing my teacher's whistle, I read out instructions I found in a library book, *Picnic Games for Children.* (Appendix 6)

Several questions ensue and I answer as best as I can. I have never personally taken part in a sack race and am excited to see how it turns out.

"Can we hang onto the sack with both hands?" I nod.

"What if I fall?"

I look around the circle. "Does this disqualify the participant?" I ask. A chorus of "nos" ensues.

"Get up and keep going," someone adds.

"Time to line up," I say. "How many sacks do we have?"

"Six," someone yells.

"Good," I say. "Lay the six sacks out along the start line and, juniors first, form six lines, one behind each sack."

This, of course, takes organization and help from older siblings. Forming lines is not something that comes naturally to young children, and after several false starts we manage to create six lines of wiggling youngsters, each three students deep. Anticipating difficulty getting into each sack, I suggest that, for these younger sets of participants, the older students may help each child into his or her sack before the race begins. For some of the youngest students the sack is as high as they are tall, and helpers fold it down so that each child can clutch the sides with both hands. One grade-two girl drops the sack immediately and bursts into tears saying it's too hard. She sits on the sidelines, and the first round is now down to five participants.

Of the five that begin, two fall almost right away, one laughing and rolling sideways and the other in tears, quitting. The two remaining students hop haphazardly along, managing, with a little help from siblings, to make it to the finish line. Everyone cheers, and, once the bags are returned to the start line, the students in the second group vehemently shake their heads when offered help getting into the sacks ahead of time. Mostly from grades three and four, these students are more confident and all six make it to the end, although two are slow and require shouts of encouragement from older students. Three grade-four boys, Paul, Trevor and Wayne, tie for first in the second group with Karen winning hands down in the third.

The grades five to eight take this race almost too seriously, and, with fierce competition from several of the boys, the first round has a three-way tie. The second round, made up exclusively of girls, has a two-way tie. Everyone flops down on the grass to rest.. When one person asks to go to the washroom and to get a drink, almost everyone follows. I make sure older siblings are supervising younger ones. Two of the mothers walk over to the washrooms, just in case.

Last weekend, after one of her friends visited for ritual afternoon tea, Rosamonde, waiting until after Bruce was in bed, told me her friend recounted that predatory males lurked in public washrooms in a nearby town, looking for young boys. Rosamonde mentioned it, in a hushed tone, telling me I must be particularly careful not to let Bruce go into a public washroom alone. In the first place, Bruce is much too young to go into a men's public washroom alone. When I questioned her for more specifics, she said that her friend wouldn't tell her something that wasn't true. The word paedophile, of course, was never uttered.

At this point in my life, I know nothing about paedophiles and, even though I feel a twinge of vague concern now when everyone traipses off to the washrooms. I don't take much stock in what seems to me to be an unsubstantiated rumour. Everyone returns and there are no incidents of any kind, except one of the stalls on the girls' side has no toilet paper.

The egg and spoon race follows the same protocol as the sack race.

I read the instructions (Appendix 7) and designate leaders, the younger children forming two teams, mostly grade threes and fours. The older group, which turns out to be girls against boys, forms four teams.

I have brought a dozen boiled eggs, somewhat of an extravagance, and hope all will go well.

Excitement runs high, even among the younger students. Older siblings give coaching tips, stressing balance and not speed. When the whistle blows, the first two participants move warily forward, hands out at sides, concentrating fiercely on the egg at the end of their spoon. They both make it to the midway finish line and back, and pass the egg and spoon on to the next. Several drop eggs along the way, and I'm glad I stipulated the "pick up" rule so that everyone can continue to be part of the race.

The seniors turn out to be even more competitive, and the girls narrowly out manoeuvre the boys. The eggs, many of them with cracked shells, are put in a bag to be taken to one student's farm to give to the pigs. After another rest and washroom-drink break, we tackle the three-legged race. The circle of students waiting for instructions is now somewhat haphazard, with a number of young bodies flopped onto their backs.

"For this race," I say, "you must pick a partner, preferably someone the same height as you." I have already asked the mothers to assist in leg-tying. "We will tie the right leg of one student to the left leg of his or her partner. You may put your arms around the other's waist."

Everyone jumps ups, and there is a lively exchange while partnerships are formed. Only a few of the youngest children decline to participate. As there are only ten younger children who have chosen to run, the mothers and I line them up and tie their legs together. This causes much giggling. In a couple of cases, the partners fall down and have to be helped up by older siblings. When I blow the whistle, an awkward and comical race ensues with several more falls. The winner is two grade four girls. In many ways, the competition is highly unfair given the age range discrepancy, however, no one seems to mind or complain, and all flop down at the finish line to untie their legs.

I know that the older group will be more of a challenge, as already the competitive nature of several has become evident. I stress fairness and that we are doing this for fun, not necessarily to win. Since all of the older group want to participate, I decide we will spread out in a much wider line, well past the markers at the beginning and end. Eight groups of two line up, most leaning forward, ready to run. When I blow the whistle, they all rush forward, one or two tripping and having to pick themselves up. As they go, everyone is laughing and yelling encouragement. It is quickly evident that several have experience in this race, with John and Keith easily taking the lead and winning by several lengths. Susie and Irene come in second.

Two of the mothers stand ready with jugs of Freshie and paper cups, and, without being told, my students line up to get a drink. Everyone's pace is slower, some complaining of sore legs and tired arms. Some drape themselves on picnic benches while others slip down to sit on the grass. One of the mothers has made cookies and passes these out to my much quieter crew. Cleaning up takes only a few minutes, and, once in my car, the three in the back seat have their eyes closed before we reach the first stop street.

Back at the school, I remind everyone to bring a game or story to share on the last day. After our afternoon baseball game, I will give out report cards. As I lock the school door, I can't believe that tomorrow will be the last day. It's something I've been waiting for and, at the same time, dreading. It's good to pick up my young son who is the one who distracts me with his chatter and enthusiasm today. In the evening, after Bruce is in bed, Rosamonde and Tante, sensing my impending ennui, carry on a cheery conversation about how exciting it will be next week for us as a family to move into our first real home.

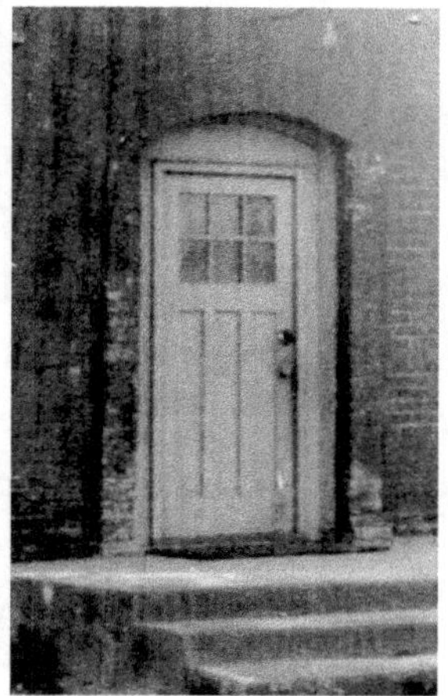

The school door

The Last Day

It's good, really, that the last day is insufferably hot and that the toilets are ranker than usual. We begin the day as we always have: everyone stands and says, "Good Morning, Mrs. Manning," followed by singing *Oh Canada* and then reciting The Lord's Prayer. There's momentary hush as everyone stares at me, wondering what I will give them to do on this last day.

As I pass out paper and pencils for the older children and crayons for the younger ones, I tell everyone, I would like them to write or draw what they plan to do over the summer holidays. I suggest a number of possibilities: a vacation somewhere, a summer job, perhaps helping around the house, fishing, swimming.

There is some sighing and one or two whispered grumblings, but they set to work. A half hour later, I ask those still writing to stop so we can share these plans. Many say little, parroting what I have already suggested, while a few read out an interesting account of what their family plans are over the summer. This includes working in the family restaurant, picking apples and other produce to be sold at the local farm market, as well as the usual list of summer holiday activities. One student proudly announces that her family has purchased a TV and that she will be watching as many programs as her parents will allow.

Partly to put in time, we take an extended recess. Afterwards, I ask those who have brought games to set them up and, for those who want to read or be read to space themselves out accordingly. They do this easily now, several older girls steering younger students into a circle, then sitting with them and reading whatever books they have. Cards, checkers and Snakes & Ladders are popular with the older group, with only a few choosing to read books they have brought. I sort through the report cards and wonder what I will do with the one for Essie Stoaker.

Just before lunch begins, one of the senior girls comes forward and asks everyone to stop, that there is a presentation about to begin. Sensing what this will be, I will have to hang on tightly to my emotions. Everyone sits up, all staring at me, several looking teary-eyed already.

At this point, the door opens and Susie and Marilyn appear, each carrying wrapped presents. When they place them on my desk, everyone begins clapping. "A going-away present," Susie says, smiling resolutely. "Something for you and your family," Marilyn adds, almost in a whisper.

"Thank you," I say, managing to keep my voice steady. "Thank you so very much." At this point, my baby decides to kick ferociously, rippling the front of my dress, distracting me from the emotionally charged moment. "I assume," I say, tugging at my dress from beneath the desk, hoping no one will notices my active belly, "you would like me to open them now."

A chorus of yeses replies.

In the first box, there is a glass jug with four matching glasses, the note saying simply, "Good luck, Mrs. Manning. We will miss you." I nod and say "thank you," again, hoping my voice is not giving me away. The second box contains two teddy bears, one large and one small, the note saying "One for your son, Bruce, and one for the new baby." Now, a few tears do spill out, and I turn briefly to wipe them away. "Bruce and our new baby to be born say thank you," I say, turning back. "It's been an amazing two years and it won't be over until after report cards this afternoon." I stand and smile at everyone. "Lunch-time. You may eat outside if you wish." The emotion in the room dissipates as lunch boxes and bags are retrieved, most staying inside to eat, a few venturing outside. Several of the older girls pull their chairs up close to mine and solemnly eat their sandwiches, saying little but looking like they want to.

"My baby," I say, "is due August twentieth." They nod, solemnly, and I can tell they hope I will say more. "We have bought a house in Scarborough on this side of Toronto," I continue, "and move in next week."

This provokes a conversation about people they know that have moved away and what it must be like. A brother and sister who were attending our school, left in March when their Dad was transferred to another town. They all say they are glad they don't have to move and then, in the same breath, reassure me it will be the best for me, especially since the school is closing. There's a lull then, even kids in rows further back pause and look wistful.

"We should be thinking about choosing teams for our ball game," I say, standing up. "Is everyone finished lunch?" There is a crumpling of waxed paper and the metal clank of lids being returned to lunch pails. Everyone files out, my senior girls chattering, about what team they want to be on.

Once teams are chosen, I throw the bat vertically into the air between the two team leaders who catch it and go hand over hand to its end to see who goes up to bat first. Even though the afternoon is hot, the game is vigorous and played with enthusiasm. Younger children are helped at bat. In some cases, when the helper holding the younger child's hands hits the ball, he scoops up the hitter and runs, carrying him or her to the base, usually not in time, but to the accompaniment of much laughter and hooting.

By three o'clock, everyone has had enough and we file back inside for report cards and goodbyes. The room becomes silent as I call out names to receive this final news, good and not so good. I haven't failed anyone but a few have low marks. As each student opens their card and reads, there is a sigh of relief. Some even pound their card and grin.

After a suitable interval, as I stand to say goodbye, the actress part of me takes over, and I smile at everyone. "This is both an ending and a beginning," I say, "not only for me but also for each one of you. I want to wish you the very best in whatever new school you attend in the fall." I know I need to move so I don't cry. I need to be positive. I walk briskly to the door. "Thank you to each and every one of you for being my students. I have learned as much and, maybe more than you have in these past two years. Have a wonderful summer holiday. Class dismissed." As I open the door and walk past the pit toilets, my sense of loss diminishes somewhat. I stand holding the front door open as students hug me and say goodbye, some in tears, some glad that summer holidays have finally begun. I watch them scatter down the road and across the field, their voices drifting back, already engaged in what lays ahead. A few stop and wave, and I wave back. It's only then that I let the tears flow. Not for long, for I must gather up my gifts and belongings, close the windows, and say my last goodbyes to this room that has consumed my life for the past two years.

I sit for a few moments looking at the empty desks, the squat black stove, the sink with its rusty water stain. Blackboards and shelves are empty except for the aged book collection in the towering mahogany bookcase. Flies buzz on the insides of the partially opened windows; the pit toilet aroma wafts in on the afternoon breeze.

I close the windows; gather up my presents and walk tentatively toward the open door, away from what was and toward what is ahead. I have survived, no, I have championed these two years. I will have my permanent teacher's certificate, and a new life is waiting.

"Goodbye," I say gently as I lock the door. "I will miss you."

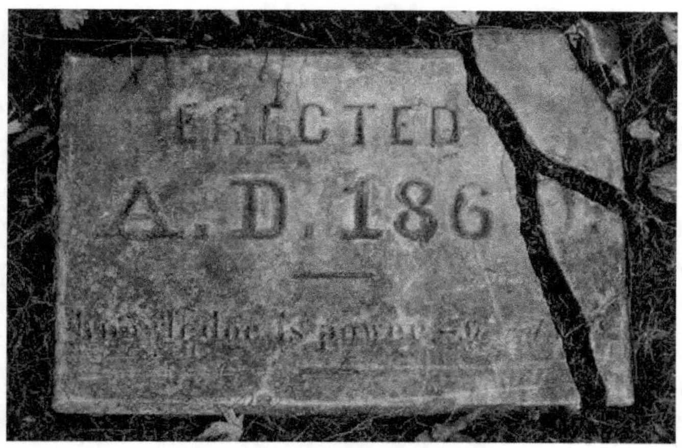

School foundation stone

Afterword

It is not until now, in writing this memoir, that I realize how much I improvised and "made do" not only in my teaching methods but also in the day-to-day events that required, often, on-the-spot decisions. I had no guidelines, no "day book" from a previous teacher to guide or give me an idea of how classes were run and what was expected of me. My only help was a vague memory from fifteen years prior, remembering how Miss Hogg organized work for the Senior grades of the then two-room Baltimore Public School.

The graded schools I visited during my teacher training were large Toronto schools with many classrooms. Most were equipped with a gymnasium, separate washrooms for boys and girls, a teachers' lunch room, a room where the nurse gave shots and where sick or injured students could be looked after and, of course, a fenced-in yard, supervised by teachers at both recess and noon hour.

In my one-room school, there were none of these facilities. The children and I ate lunch together; all other activities took place within its four walls. The most glaring difference, of course, was the fact that I rarely ventured into the yard at recess or noon hour. The students were on their own, and whatever bullying, fighting, name-calling, discrimination that took place there was settled somehow. I highly discouraged tattling and, in this era of absolute teacher control, if some obvious misdeed was brought to my attention, such as the smoking incident, it is likely the children involved would have been disciplined, again at home.

Preparation time and classroom routine were also radically different in my school. Although preparation time for Ontario teachers did not come into being until the early 1990's, teachers in graded schools were usually working on courses for one or two grades. There were course outlines, seatwork examples, and reference books to help the novice teacher. I had none of these, and with no one to advise me, I forged ahead on my own, creating a schedule and modifying it as time and situation allowed. In my first year of teaching, I spent two to three hours on weekday evenings, and up to ten hours each weekend, going through textbooks, writing out seatwork questions, and planning the next week's courses. Each morning, I arrived at the school by 7:30 a.m. in order to have time to write out on the blackboards the questions I had composed the night before. I would also list the day's agenda, the grade and subject I would be working with each half hour or so. Often, in the afternoon, senior students who had finished their day's work, would listen to juniors read and drill basic spelling and math concepts.

I don't recall having to deal with a sick student. There was no telephone in the school. In an emergency, Marilyn would go across the road to her house and make a phone call. Most students walked or biked to school, and, if a given student was not feeling well, they would have to wait until dismissal time when an older sibling or student could walk them home. "If you don't feel well, fold your arms on your desk and rest your head," was the general rule.

Cleanliness was basic and we "made do" with what we had. Hand-washing after using the pit toilets was mandatory, but I'm sure some managed to evade the soap and cold water, slipping back to their desk while I was engrossed with other students. In the winter and on rainy days, coats and boots were a challenge. If the stove was going, they would be on the backs of chairs as close to the heat as possible.

I know that the cap gun incident would have been treated with much more severity than I gave it. In the 1960`s, rural schools had never heard of lock downs or police intervention when a cap gun was found on the premises. It was to me, an annoying situation, and I dealt with it.

Whether or not, any parents were told about it, I have no idea and think it unlikely. It was kid stuff and kept that way.

Some unorthodox things I did out of necessity, some because the opportunity presented itself, and, being both teacher and principal, I could do what I wanted. I'm sure our humanitarian science project, Rebel the Starling, would not, in a graded school, have been given the leeway it had with us. It didn't occur to me that allowing a partly-grown bird to fly about the classroom was stepping outside any rules. It happened, and we dealt with it.

I was aware that my pregnancy would not have been tolerated in a graded school. I don't know if any of my students talked to their parents about my expanding middle. and I suppose, on weekends, I might have seen parents at a store or on the street. No one seemed concerned, and it wasn't until the second-year inspector made his derogatory comments that I thought much about it. By then, of course, it didn't matter. School was nearly over.

In spite of the work load and physical shortcomings, these two years stand out as exceptional, definitely worth remembering and writing about, an almost sixty-year-past slice of rural history in southern Ontario.

Appendix

1. Some of you might remember these primary printing books. Each contained pages with widely spaced lines, three in a grouping with the middle line being a broken line. The bottom half of a lowercase letter went below the dotted line, the upper half above. In contrast, uppercase letters were to be placed between the two sold lines. Each page had a letter in the top left, uppercase on the left page and lowercase on the page opposite. The dutiful young student was required to fill the pages with replicas of this first letter, over and over. Some didn't seem to mind the boring repetition and would labour away to make each letter as perfect as possible. Others, like me back in 1946—Charleswood, Manitoba Public School—hated the exercise and went as fast as possible, speeding up as the wretched letters accumulated.

2. The New Math concept that annoys me the most is that of teaching long-division, especially to students who, at the end of grade three, were introduced to the traditional method requiring the student to look for "the highest common denominator." Using this former method, if you are dividing 23 into 476, you look for the largest multiple of 23 that will fit into 476. Twenty is that number and so you subtract 460 from 476, leaving a remainder of 13. The answer is 20 with a remainder of 13.

The New Math discards the highest common denominator and asks the student to keep subtracting 23 from 476 to see how many times it will go. The problem with this is that it sets up more opportunities to make errors to say nothing of not understanding the process in the first place.

3. Stage blocking involves telling each actor where and when to move during his or her lines. The actor writes "the blocking" into his/her script so that all movement is smooth and natural. The blocking is incorporated into the actor's lines and memory.

4. From an internet site called, grandma ideas/fox and geese, the following explanation of the game is given: To play this wintry game, make paths through the snow in the shape of a wagon wheel. Stamp down a four-foot circle in the centre of the wheel. This is home—a safe zone for the geese. Select one person to be the fox (it). The rest of the players are geese.

The fox chases the geese along the trails in the snow. All players must stay on the trails at all times. Players cannot jump from one trail to a different one. Geese may run into 'home' for a momentary rest where they will be safe. The fox cannot tag them if the geese are in the 'home' circle. However, the geese cannot stay there very long. After a minute or two, they must leave the home circle. The fox cannot enter the home circle nor can he or she tag any geese that are in the 'safe' home circle. He or she may run through the circle in pursuit of a goose if the goose keeps running through the circle and doesn't stop inside it.

When the fox tags a goose, their roles are reversed. The goose now becomes the fox and the fox becomes a goose. The new fox begins chasing the geese trying to tag one of them. Play continues until (a) everybody gets too tired (b) everybody gets soggy, wet, and cold (c) the fox gets frustrated because he or she can't tag anybody and he is IT all of the time (d) all of the above!

5. Practice teaching is the term used at Teachers' College for the days we were sent out in twos to allotted classroom schools where, from Monday to Thursday, we each taught for one hour and, on Fridays, we taught for a half day. I don't remember how many sessions we had over the school year. We also had one rural week where this pattern was repeated. None of this prepared us adequately for full-time teaching.

6. Sack race Instructions:

When the whistle is blown, participants will run to the sack, put both feet in and begin hopping toward the finish line. Contestants must keep both feet in their sack and, at least, one hand on the sack at all times. The sack must remain as close to the waist as possible and should not fall below the knees. The first racer to the finish line wins.

7. Spoon and egg race instructions:

Divide players into teams and line the teams up. Pass out a spoon and egg to each person in the front of the line. Blow the whistle, signalling the start of the relay. Each person with a spoon and egg must carry the egg on the spoon to and from the finish line. (I add that dropped eggs can be picked up, the team member continuing). As soon as the player returns to the line, he or she passes the egg and spoon on to the next person in line.

The winning team receives a prize.

Author Bio

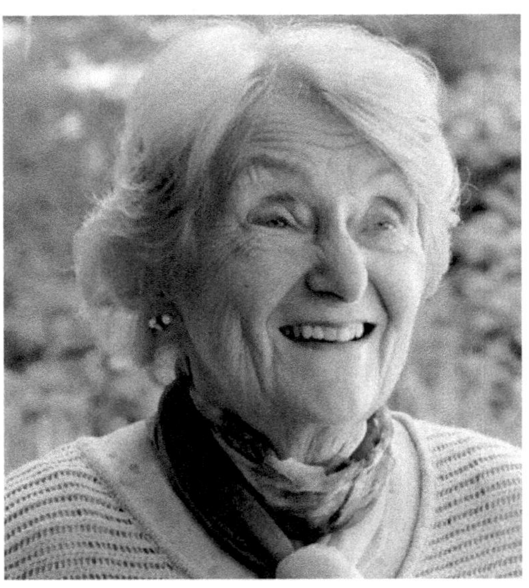

Linda Hutsell-Manning's writing career spans thirty-five years and includes an impressive variety of genres including poetry, plays, TV, short fiction and novels. Born in Winnipeg, Manitoba in 1940, she moved to Ontario at age nine and, after Ryerson Polytechnical Institute and Toronto Teachers' College, taught for two years in a one-room school between Cobourg and Port Hope, Ontario. Following this, she attended the University of Guelph as a mature student, graduating with a B.A. in 1975. Encouraged by two of her university professors, she began writing full time in 1981.

She has worked as a free-lance journalist; taught creative writing at several community colleges and hosted an author reading series. In the first twenty years, she published primarily juvenile fiction including three picture books, three juvenile plays, two time-travel novels and scripts for TVO's Polka Dot Door. During this time, she gave countless school/library workshops across Canada as well as in Germany and Luxembourg.

In 2011, her literary novel, *That Summer in Franklin*, was published by Second Story Press. Its sequel, *The Tangling of Years*, is waiting to be published. In 2017, a novella, *Heads I Win, Tails You Lose*, was short-listed in a Quattro Books novella competition. Her two-act comedy, *A Certain Singing Teacher* premiered in 2017. She is currently working on a novella/short story collection, *Whatever Were You Thinking When You Did That?* and a poetry collection, *Falling into Light*.

She has lived in many Canadian communities from Kamloops, BC to Cobourg, Ontario, where she now makes her home, writing in the attic office of a century farmhouse. More information about Linda's publications can be found at www.lindahutsellmanning.ca

Acknowledgements

During my three years researching and writing this book, I received help from a wide range of people: students I interviewed, many of whose names appear in the book; people I contacted through social media who gave me invaluable information, and others whose contributions are listed below.

Kate Sureras for the photo of Cold Springs Hall.

Mark Edwardson for converting1964 Oklahoma slides to digital.

Cobourg Yesteryears for those who shared Mother's Day stories.

Anne Sanders for advice re small pox needle.

Port Hope historical Society (Tim & Patricia Austin) for Burley bus photo.

Bernadette Gatien for valuable information re Burley bus school trip.

Kathryn Huck, Downtown Photography, for school stone and location photos.

Tracy Mallon-Jensen, AGO, for advice re Star Weekly photograph.

Maia-Mari Sutnik, AGO, for advice re Star Weekly photograph.

Dorothy Lambeth for 2006 permission to use Star Weekly photograph.

Nancy Moore for reading an early version of the manuscript.

Karen Murray for permission to photograph school date stone on her patio.

Judy Baker for 1964 photo of school and yard taken by her aunt Jessie Pratt.

Jill Edwards for copy of Oklahoma program.

And any other contributor I may have missed!

I would like to give special thanks to my publisher and editor Shane Joseph for believing this memoir has potential and for his astute editing and suggestions.

Finally, I would like to thank my family: my husband James who read early drafts and offered editing advice, my adult children Bruce, David and Laura who all provided invaluable support as I was researching and writing.